Table of Contents

DEDICATION
For Laureen

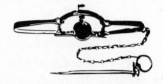

Introduction

MOUNTAIN MEN: the courageous and mythical folk who opened the West. In the face of hostile Natives, unknown territory and assured deprivation, these hardy men abandoned their eastern homes for the backwoods of North America. Each man had his own story, and those stories often echoed similar themes. Mountain men were drawn west more than they were pushed. As boys they dreamed of adventure, and as men they lived it. They hunted bear in thick forests, trapped beaver in icy streams and engaged Natives in enduring battles for life and land. Most were fiercely independent and intent on carving out a life that shouted their determined character to the world.

Such shouts went mostly unheard because mountain men were drawn to country where none of their own kind lived. Folks knew of the mountain men. Their stories were popular fare in eastern cities, and most were celebrities even though they didn't know it. Nor would they have cared. The mountain men scoffed at fooferaw, the catchall term they used to disdainfully describe the trappings of civilized life. A buckskin outfit, a rifle, a sharp knife and, for some, a trap were all they

MOUNTAIN
⚬ MEN ⚬

Frontier Adventurers
Alone Against the Wilderness

TONY HOLLIHAN

FOLK
LORE
PUBLISHING

The Publisher: Folklore Publishing
Website: www.folklorepublishing.com

National Library of Canada Cataloguing in Publication

> Hollihan, K. Tony (Kelvin Tony), 1964–
> Mountain men : frontier adventurers alone against the wilderness
> / K. Tony Hollihan.
>
> (Legends series)
> Includes bibliographical references.
> ISBN 1-894864-09-3

1. Adventure and adventurers—United States—Biography. 2. Pioneers—United States—Biography. 3. Frontier and pioneer life—United States. 4. Adventure and adventurers—Canada—Biography. 5. Pioneers—Canada—Biography. 6. Frontier and pioneer life—Canada. I. Title. II. Series: Legends series (Edmonton, Alta.)
F592.H64 2004   973'.09'9   C2003-906763-7

Project Director: Faye Boer
Copy Editor: Andrea Emberley
Cover Image: Circa Arts—American West. Image Club Graphic. #67. © 1997
Photography credits: Every effort has been made to accurately credit the sources of photographs. Any errors or omissions should be directed to the publisher for changes in future editions. *Photographs courtesy of* Church of Jesus Christ of Latter-Day Saints (p. 80, P328); Colorado Springs Pioneers Museum (p.111); Glenbow Archives, Calgary, Canada (p. 129, NA-1274-19; p. 203, NA-1315-28; p. 212, NA-619-2; p. 216, NA-2373-15; p. 220, NA-249-99); Hudson's Bay Company Archives, Archives of Manitoba (p.137, HBCA1938/107/1; Joselyn Art Museum (p.157); Kansas State Historical Society (p. 83; p. 146); Library of Congress (p. 26, USZ62-1431; p. 34, USZ62-112549; p. 42, USZ62-93521; p. 58, USZ62-7368; p. 75, USZ62-908; p. 77, USZ62-102134; p.183, USZ62-107503; p. 194, LC-DIG-cwpbh-00514); Missouri Historical Society (p. 100); National Archives of Canada (title page, C-2771; p. 114, C-29925); Oregon Historical Society (p. 123, OrHi 407); Nevada State Historical Society (p.105); Richard Frajola (p.102); Saskatchewan Archives Board (p. 118, R-A24431); Taos Historic Museums (p. 177, G2/4; p.185, G2/104); Washington University Gallery of Art, St. Louis. Gift of Nathaniel Phillips, 1890 (p. 20).

We acknowledge the support of the Alberta Foundation for the Arts for our publishing program.

COMMITTED TO THE DEVELOPMENT OF CULTURE AND THE ARTS

needed. And a campfire around which to tell or listen to a tale as large as the vast expanses that surrounded them.

Mountain men were always found at the leading edge of western expansion, and it was their resolution that opened the North American continent. In the late 18th century, they pushed across the Appalachian Mountains. A generation later, they led the charge over the Rocky Mountains. Their journeys were lonely, usually taken with a handful of dependable men at most, but those who measured elbowroom in miles rather than feet would have it no other way. They were so tied to the open west that when it began to fill with settlers in the 1840s, the mountain men began to vanish.

This book explores the lives of eight mountain men.

Daniel Boone longed for open spaces and led the way for settlement in Kentucky. Boone spent most of his life on the fringe of the American frontier, but it wasn't without cost. He fought the Natives and the British, was captured several times and lost children to violent deaths. Because of shifting frontier boundaries Boone lost most of his land claims and his fortune, but he was a man of principal who would not rest until he had paid his debts.

Davy Crockett's homespun ways and larger-than-life image endeared him to Americans. His military career saw him rise from a volunteer to a lieutenant colonel. His earthy and funny yarns and his straight-shooting ways were popular with electors who regularly voted him into office. But Crockett was always more comfortable in the woods hunting bear. He explored Tennessee and traveled throughout Florida and Texas, where he put up a brave final front against Santa Anna at the Alamo.

James Bridger listened to the tales of river men and trappers in St. Louis and dreamed of a life adventuring in the Rocky Mountains. He got his chance with the Henry-Ashley expedition in 1822 and went on to spend 20 years trapping and exploring the mysterious West. In later years his reputation as a guide was so great that the United States Army regularly called upon him for his services. Known for spinning tall tales, Bridger was also a stubborn man who locked horns with the Blackfoot, Sioux, Mormons and, occasionally, with his military employers.

James Beckwourth was born a slave but went on to become a much sought-after trader, Crow war chief and militia captain, or so he claimed. Beckwourth was known for his exaggeration and self-aggrandizement, but he did live a full life. He lived with the Crow as an agent of the Upper Missouri Outfit; he fought the Seminole in Florida; he opened Beckwourth's Pass through the Sierra Nevada; and he owned and operated several successful businesses in his life.

Peter Skene Ogden was so taken by stories of trappers and explorers that he rejected a career in law to pursue a life similar to theirs. He worked his way up the hierarchy of the powerful Hudson's Bay Company and led a series of successful expeditions into the Snake River country of the Pacific Northwest. Throughout the late 1820s, his presence in the Oregon Territory was enough to keep the region from falling into American hands. Courageous, impartial and duty bound, Ogden enjoyed the respect of his superiors, American and Russian competitors and Natives.

Jedidiah Smith read of Lewis and Clark's western adventures as a child and signed on with the Henry-Ashley expedition as a young man to forge his own trails west. Within one year, his employers identified Smith as one of their best assets and directed him to explore west of the Rocky Mountains. Later, he formed his own operation with Bill Sublette and David Jackson, but he was always more of a mountain man than a businessman. Smith's travels unlocked the famed South Pass, took him west into Spanish California, north into British North America, and did much to open the far west to settlement.

Christopher "Kit" Carson escaped the binds of an apprenticeship so he could see the western lands spoken of so fondly by traders and mountain men doing business at his master's saddlery. His home was Taos, New Mexico, but he trapped in Sioux and Blackfoot country to the north and came to know of the Natives' fighting abilities firsthand. When the bottom fell out of trapping in the 1840s, he signed on as a guide with Captain John Fremont's western exploratory expeditions and found himself knee-deep in the Mexican War. Carson's word was as respected as the western sky was big, and he rarely failed to earn the admiration of those he encountered.

John George "Kootenai" Brown fled Ireland as a young man so that he could pursue adventure in North America. Brown lived a varied life, prospecting for gold, riding as an express rider for the United States Army, trading with Natives and hunting buffalo throughout mid-western and western North America. Eventually, he settled down in what was known as the Kootenay Lakes region in the eastern foothills of the Rocky Mountains, where he became a legend promoting conservation.

Here are their stories.

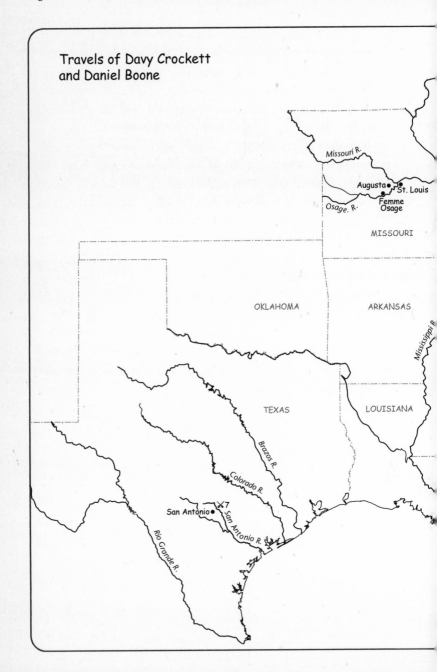

Travels of Davy Crockett
and Daniel Boone

Missouri R.

Augusta ● ● St. Louis
● Femme
Osage. R. Osage

MISSOURI

OKLAHOMA

ARKANSAS

Mississippi R.

TEXAS

LOUISIANA

Brazos R.

Colorado R.

San Antonio ● ✕7
San Antonio R.

Rio Grande R.

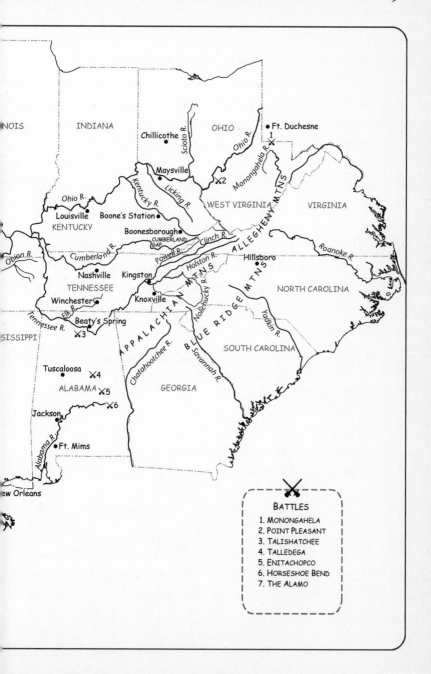

BATTLES

1. MONONGAHELA
2. POINT PLEASANT
3. TALISHATCHEE
4. TALLEDEGA
5. ENITACHOPCO
6. HORSESHOE BEND
7. THE ALAMO

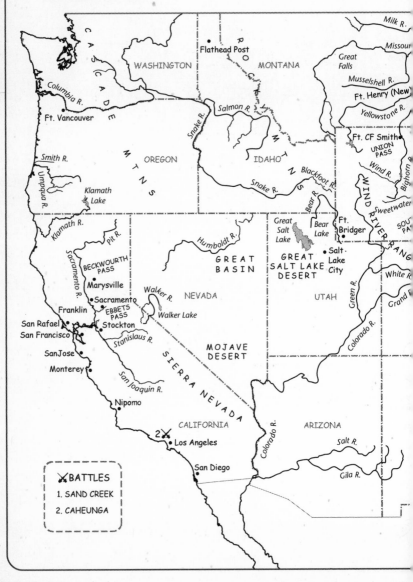

Travels of Jim Bridger, James Beckwourth, Kit Carson and Jedidiah Smith

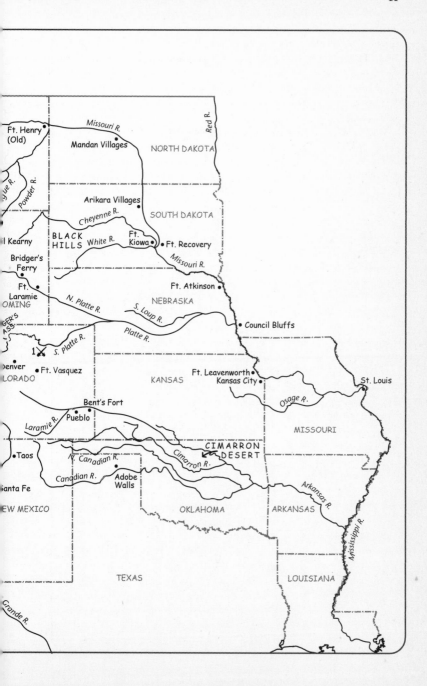

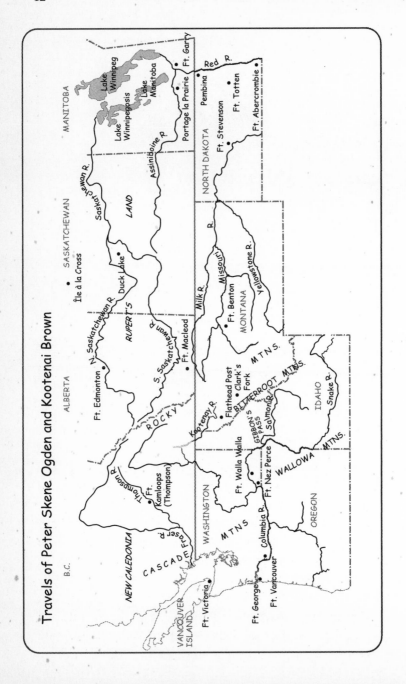

Travels of Peter Skene Ogden and Kootenai Brown

CHAPTER ONE

Daniel Boone
1734–1820

SQUIRE BOONE WAS 18 YEARS OLD in 1712 when he signed on as a cabin boy and sailed across the Atlantic Ocean. His father, George Boone, was a member of the Society of Friends—the Quakers—and he had tired of religious persecution in England. He'd heard that a man might live free from oppression in the New World. The rumors that land was cheap there also appealed to George. But while he was willing to make a change in the best interest of his family, he wouldn't do it based on idle talk. Instead, George sent Squire and two other children west to confirm the stories. A few years later, the three sent word that the rumors were true, and in 1717, George took the rest of his family to the British colonies in North America. They arrived in Philadelphia in October and soon settled near Abington, just north of Philadelphia, where they joined the Gwynedd Meeting of Quakers.

Squire married Sarah Morgan in 1720, and they moved to Oley, Pennsylvania, where he worked as a weaver and occasional farmer. Daniel, their sixth child, was born there on October 22, 1734. As a child Daniel helped around the farm, tended the family's small dairy herd and learned something of working iron in his father's smithy. But Dan loved the backwoods, where he enjoyed his leisure time and occasionally escaped to avoid his chores. When he was 10 years old he'd disappear into the woods for days at a time, taking with him his "herdsman's club," a short, sharpened sapling that he used as a spear. Squire encouraged the budding woodsman by giving Dan his first short-barreled rifle at age 12. Dan responded by ensuring that the family's larder was never empty.

Dan was more comfortable scouting the Flying Hills and the Neversink Mountains than he was seated on the knotty pine bench of the country school, so he didn't suffer the stuffy classroom long. After an especially harsh beating from his teacher, he fled the school and never returned. His uncle continued to tutor him in composition, but soon gave up in despair. Book learning simply wasn't Dan's strength, and his father wasn't going to hold it against the boy.

"It's no great matter," concluded Squire. "Let the girls do the spelling, and Dan will do the hunting."

Dan knew that his father wouldn't accept his fondness for mischief as much as his love of the woods, so the boy was careful to keep from Squire those pranks he knew would result in punishment. Many a local farmer scratched his head in the early morning as he looked at his barn and saw the pieces of his disassembled wagon hanging high. Others did more than scratch. On one occasion, a neighbor named George Wilcoxen, who was unfamiliar with firearms, came to Squire for advice on deer hunting. Squire lent him a long musket and loaded it so it would be ready for use the next day. Secretly, Dan and a friend withdrew the ball and added six charges of powder. But troubled by guilt, they worried that the musket might explode and injure the man. Guilt turned to fear when they heard the uncommonly loud crack of the rifle the following morning.

They found George with a mottled hanky held to his blood-ied and bruised face as he rushed past them to find Squire.

"The kick from the musket knocked me to the ground, and my face struck a rock," explained George.

"No," protested Squire. "The load in the musket was so small that you could have rested its breech on your nose and fired without the least danger."

Anxious to change the subject, Dan interrupted.

"Did you kill a deer?"

"Well, I had a fair shot, but the force of the blast was so strong that I didn't notice if it struck the animal. But it was," he added, "a dear shot!"

Relieved to hear that George retained his sense of humor, Dan and his friend hurried off to look for the deer, which they found and retrieved. The strange injury was soon forgotten, but George loaded his own musket thereafter.

In the late 1740s, the Boones fell out of favor with the local Quakers. Two of Squire's daughters married outside the society, and as a result, he was judged unfit for membership and expelled. Life was difficult for an outsider in the tightly knit community, and in the spring of 1750 Squire and his family left Pennsylvania. They moved south, stopping briefly in Vir-ginia and eventually settled in North Carolina's Yadkin Valley. Twenty-year-old Dan was enthusiastic about the move. Although his father had purchased land to farm, Dan turned his eye to hunting. And because the Yadkin Valley was on the western edge of settlement, Dan didn't have to look far. He was soon shooting more than 30 deer a day and selling what the family didn't need in local Salisbury. At a time when an average hunter might kill a half dozen deer on a good day, Dan's take was remarkable, and soon folks were shaking their heads at his proficiency.

In 1754, only a few years after the Boones arrived in the Yadkin Valley, the French and Indian Wars erupted. Since the

17th century, the French had controlled the interior of North America, but British colonists were eager to settle west of the Appalachian Mountains. It wasn't just a matter of slipping over the range. The French had a string of forts stretching from the Great Lakes to the Gulf of Mexico, and they enjoyed good relations with the Natives. The French and the Natives traded for furs in a way that required few Frenchmen and allowed Natives to live much as they always had because French practices did not intrude on Native lifestyles. The British, however, wanted to establish settlements and to clear land for farming. Such practices undermined traditional Native ways, and the Natives were quick to oppose the British by allying with their old trading partners, the French.

Dan enlisted as a teamster with Major Edward Dobbs' militia company, which fought with General Edward Braddock's regular troops. Braddock's orders were to drive the French out of the Ohio Valley and into Canada. In July 1755, he marched his 1400 men on Fort Duquesne (present-day Pittsburgh). Aware that they could not hold the fort against such numbers, the French and Natives advanced to surround Braddock's men, raining down intense sniper fire on the British. Within hours, 900 British soldiers were killed or wounded. Braddock called a retreat, which proved difficult because their wagons were at the rear of the column. Chaos ensued, and Braddock was mortally wounded. The Battle of the Monongahela was a disaster for the British.

Dan was about a half mile from the front when the French attack began, and he joined the retreat when it was ordered. After he forded the Monongahela River, he was relieved to see that the enemy had chosen to raid the abandoned wagons and scalp the dead rather than continue their pursuit. Dan blamed Braddock for the defeat. He knew that the general's refusal to use Native scouts to observe the enemies' activities was a mistake. Over the years he had learned enough from Natives to respect their skills in the woods, and he was certain that the Delaware allies of the British would have warned them of the advancing enemy. Instead, Braddock alienated the Delaware by telling their chief that any land taken from the French would be reserved for white settlement. The Delaware withdrew to let the arrogant British suffer their fate.

The best that came from Dan's introduction to frontier warfare was a friendship with John Finley. Finley made his living trading with the Natives in Kentucky, and his stories of blue grass, abundant game and open spaces to the west enthralled Dan. Perhaps he even considered heading west then, but Dan rejoined his family in the Yadkin Valley, where a romance blossomed with Rebecca Bryan, one of his brothers-in-law's sisters. Dan met 16-year-old Rebecca in late 1753, and his attraction to her was immediate, but he was eager to know something of the young woman's character. A cherry-picking party provided him that opportunity. The pair slipped away from their companions and relaxed in the cool shade of an oak tree. Dan unsheathed his knife and slashed at the grass, extending the arc of his stroke until he cut Rebecca's fine white apron. The apparently careless action was designed "to try her temper," as Dan put it. Her reaction was a smile and Dan knew he had found his wife. Soon after that he shot a deer, took it to her house and dressed it, a frontier custom designed to demonstrate a man's ability as a provider. Her family was impressed, and the couple was married on August 14, 1756.

In the decade that followed, Dan enlisted a few times to fight the Natives, but he was more preoccupied with the explorations that were to contribute to his fame. He traveled into eastern Tennessee, where he carved his name on a tree as was his practice, and he hunted in western North Carolina. Then, in the summer of 1765 he joined Major John Field's Florida expedition. Britain had recently acquired the territory from Spain, and the government was offering free land to Protestant

immigrants. Dan was eager to leave the Yadkin Valley, which
had become increasingly popular with settlers. He saw the
expedition as an opportunity to scout out a new home. Unfortunately, the party almost starved in Florida and was saved only
by the goodwill of some Seminoles. The swamps, reptiles and
bugs that overran so much of the territory were none too
appealing, but the challenges didn't deter Dan from purchas-
ing land in Pensacola. Returning home on December 25, he
informed Rebecca of his intentions to move south. She flatly
refused to go. Dan would have to look elsewhere to ease his
wanderlust.

Dan continued his search over the next few years. He
hunted in Tennessee and traveled down the Mississippi River to
New Orleans to sell his furs. Unfortunately, Dan and his party
lost much of their earnings when Creek warriors attacked them
as they returned north. Dan finally turned his sights to Kentucky, despite the British Royal Proclamation of 1763 that forbade western settlement in the region. The British government
had decided that the territory between the Appalachian Mountains and the Mississippi River would be reserved for Natives.
Dan was one among many—including colonial govern-
ments—who ignored such restraints. In the fall of 1767, Dan,
his brother Squire and William Hill crossed the Blue Ridge and
the Allegheny Mountains. Dan shot his first buffalo just west of
the Cumberland Mountains, and he made his way back to the
Yadkin Valley at winter's end without realizing he'd actually
been in the land described by his old friend John Finley. By
1768, he had returned to Kentucky three times, thoroughly
enjoying the abundance of game and the absence of settlers.

Dan did more than hunt in Kentucky. He acted as an agent
for Judge Richard Henderson, a land speculator operating out
of Hillsboro, North Carolina, who financed Dan's excursions
in return for information about the region. In May 1769, Dan
began his most ambitious expedition into Kentucky. Interest in

the region had been heightened since the signing of the 1768
Treaty of Stanwix, which saw the Iroquois cede much of what
would become Kentucky. Although settlers and land specula-
tors were pleased with the transaction, the Shawnee and
Cherokee, who also claimed the territory, raided to demonstrate their displeasure. With Henderson's backing, Dan, his
brother-in-law John Stuart, John Finley and a few others
headed north along the Powell River and through the Cumberland Gap, eventually reaching the Warrior's Path—a Native
trail that snaked into the Kentucky hunting grounds. The
Warrior's Path was well used by Natives, and it was inevitable
that Dan's party would encounter them as they did in late
December. Dan and his brother-in-law were hunting when
a party of Shawnee led by a warrior known to the English as Will
Emery, but called Captain Will, approached and demanded
to be taken to their camp. Outnumbered, the pair agreed. The
Shawnee stole just about everything, leaving the party with
only a rifle and two pair of moccasins each.

"Brothers, go home and stay there," advised Captain Will as
his braves disappeared into the woods. "This is Shawnee hunting ground, and all the animals, skins and furs are ours."

Dan wasn't about to see six months of work lost, so he convinced John Stuart to join him in tracking the Shawnee. At the
very least, he wanted to retrieve his horses. The two caught up
with the braves and made off with five horses. A day later,
while they rested the animals after long hours of hard riding,
the Shawnee swooped down on them, captured Dan and John
and resumed their journey back to their village on the Ohio
River. A week later, the pair managed to escape by slipping into
a thick cane patch. When they returned to their camp and
found it deserted, they resigned themselves to a long, exhaust-
ing journey back to North Carolina. Fortunately, they found
their companions 40 miles later. The reunion was happy; all
had thought the two men dead. Dan was also happy to see

George Caleb Bingham, *Daniel Boone Escorting Settlers through the Cumberland Gap*, 1851–52. Oil on canvas, 36.5 x 50.25. Washington University Gallery of Art, St. Louis. Gift of Nathaniel Phillips, 1890.

Squire, who had arrived with more horses, traps and ammunition. Dan, Squire and John Stuart decided to remain in the territory to trap, but they agreed to stay clear of the Warrior's Path. Such caution did not help Stuart. He disappeared along the Rockcastle River, and although his remains were discovered years later, the cause of his death was a mystery.

In the fall of 1773, Dan made the dangerous decision to settle in Kentucky. He had spent the better part of the previous five years there, hunting, trapping and exploring as far west as the Falls of the Ohio (present-day Louisville). In 1771, Natives again raided he and his brother while they were camped in the Powell Valley, and they lost furs and supplies accumulated over the previous six months. It was a particular blow to Dan, who had been slowly paying off his creditors. Suddenly, he faced an even greater debt. But his travels gave him confidence that Kentucky was the land of opportunity, and he was certain that he could meet his financial obligations and even prosper there. Others shared his optimism, and when the Boones boarded up their cabins, loaded their packhorses and said goodbye to the Yadkin Valley, five families joined them. However, high spirits plummeted when the party separated near the Powell Valley. The Shawnee attacked and killed six men, including Dan's son James. When the rest of the party learned of the deaths, they returned to Kentucky despite Dan's objections.

Another delay was forced upon Dan in 1774, when the Ohio Valley erupted in the bloody conflict known as Dunmore's War. Tensions between Natives and white settlers had been mounting in the region since the signing of the Treaty of Fort Stanwix, and they finally boiled over in 1774, when settlers killed the family of Mingo chief John Logan. Lord Dunmore, governor of Virginia, organized a militia of 1500 men to march on the Native villages along the Scioto River. But he wanted to find and warn government employees who were scattered throughout Kentucky surveying the land ceded by the Iroquois of the impending war. The responsibility to choose men for the dangerous task fell upon Captain William Russell. Russell immediately thought of Boone, whom he knew from the failed 1773 expedition to Kentucky.

Russell wrote to his superior, "If they are alive, it is indisputable that Boone must find them."

Dan, together with Michael Stoner, spent two months traveling 800 miles to warn those in Kentucky of the approaching conflict. When the mission was complete, Dan was commissioned as a lieutenant in the colonial militia. He raised a company of men and quickly proved his value by reducing Native raids in the Clinch River valley region. He was promoted to captain and placed in command of Blackmore's, Cowan's and Moore's forts, which were all under siege by Logan's braves. When the Shawnee suffered defeat at the Battle of Point Pleasant in October, Chief Cornstalk agreed to the Treaty of Camp Charlotte, which established the Ohio River as the western boundary of white settlement.

Dunmore's War was over, and Dan and his men were discharged. The timing was opportune. Land speculator Richard Henderson was finally in a position to pursue his dream of creating the 14th colony of Transylvania in Kentucky and Tennessee. His Transylvania Land Company was prepared to buy 20 million acres of land in the region, and in the fall of 1874, he traveled to Kentucky to verify Dan's claim that the Cherokee were willing to sell. He was pleased to discover that Dan hadn't been exaggerating. Following negotiations that saw Dan establish the boundaries of the purchase, the Treaty of Sycamore Shoals was signed on March 17, 1775. For $10,000 worth of goods, the Transylvania Land Company purchased 200,000 acres between the Kentucky and Cumberland rivers. "The Great Grant," as it was known, was followed by a "Path Grant," which allowed Henderson's company to cut a road through the mountains of southwest Virginia to the Cumberland Gap.

Unfortunately for Henderson, the purchase was illegal because it transgressed the 1763 Royal Proclamation that forbade private land purchases from Natives. At the time, however, Henderson appeared to have struck a great deal. Still some Natives opposed the sale, and many of those who supported it did so reluctantly. Oconostota, head chief of the Cherokee, gave Dan a warning.

"Brother, we have given you a fine land, but I believe you will have much trouble in settling it." Oconostota was referring to the northern tribes, who would not readily abandon their traditional hunting grounds.

Dan headed for the Long Island of Holston (present-day Kingston), where he was in charge of surveying and cutting the Wilderness Road that would give settlers easy access to the company's land holdings. He met Squire there, who informed Dan that he'd left the Yadkin Valley none too soon. In early March, a creditor had won a judgment against Dan, and the sheriff had come to his house to arrest him.

But in late March, Dan had reason to think he might have been better off taking his chances with the sheriff. A letter he wrote to Henderson detailed the dangers of carving out the Wilderness Road:

> On March the 25 a party of Indians fired on my company about half an hour before day, and killed Mr. Tweety and his Negro, and wounded Mr. Walker very deeply but I hope he will recover. On March the 28 as we were hunting for provisions, we found Samuel Tate's son, who gave us an account that the Indians fired on their camp on the 27 day. My brother and I went down and found two men killed and sculped, Thomas McDowell and Jeremiah McPfeeters. I have sent a man down to all the lower companies in order to gather them all to the mouth of Otter Creek…where we shall immediately erect a fort.

Dan urged Henderson to hurry in with reinforcements. Henderson, aware that the success of his enterprise depended on Dan's ability to build the Wilderness Road and to attract settlers, hurried to meet with his key agent. The journey was difficult, and many of his party deserted because they refused to travel in a region beset by Native troubles. By the time Henderson

arrived in late April, Dan's men were already building Fort
Boone. The site was on the south side of the Kentucky River,
downstream from the mouth of Otter Creek. Dan had chosen
the location because of a nearby salt lick, which attracted game
and provided salt. Henderson renamed the fort Boonesborough
and envisioned it as the capital of Transylvania.

Henderson wasted little time in calling into session a general assembly of representatives from the communities in the
Transylvania Land Company's purchase. On May 23 they met
under the "divine elm" at Boonesborough to make laws and
establish a government. Dan and five others represented
Boonesborough. Dan proposed two laws, one to preserve game
and the other to improve the quality of horse breeds. But those
who didn't recognize the Transylvania Land Company's purchase or Henderson's authority voiced their opposition. The
anger of Henderson's opponents heightened when he proposed that settlers be forced to rent rather than own property.
Months later, Henderson was selling large tracts of land to
friends at low prices while charging settlers exorbitant rental
fees and withholding some of the best land for his close
friends. The practices further upset many of the settlers who
had hoped to prohibit such land speculation by requiring
those who bought the land to work it.

In June, Dan traveled to the Yadkin Valley to collect his family
and move them to Boonesborough. He returned in September,
leading 20 additional settlers that he had recruited. Henderson
and his partners voted to give Dan a gift of 2000 acres "with the
thanks of the Proprietors, for the exemplary services he has ren-
dered to the Company." Dan surveyed and selected a 1000-acre
site on Tate's Creek, southwest of Boonesborough. The settlers
who followed Dan were the first of a few hundred who arrived
throughout the fall of 1775. But what started as a promising
flow turned to a trickle as a renewed wave of frontier violence
rolled through Kentucky. The American Revolution had erupted.

The Natives who lived in the region were eager to stem the tide of western settlement, and they allied with the British who promised to maintain a Native homeland west of the Appalachian Mountains.

As Native raiding increased, Boonesborough endured a terrifying episode that brought Chief Oconostota's dire prediction back to mind. In July 1776, braves captured Jemima Boone, Dan's 14-year-old daughter, and her friends Betsy and Fanny Calloway, when they wandered away from the community. The girls' screams alerted those in the fort, and Dan was among the first to respond. A search party was hurriedly assembled, and Dan took the lead. Their work was made easier by the girls' ingenuity; they broke twigs on trees to signal the direction they had walked and delayed the Natives as much as possible. The Boonesborough men found the braves three days later, attacked the camp and freed the uninjured girls. News of the incident spread quickly across the frontier, and Dan's leadership role did much to enhance his reputation as a skilled and fearless woodsman.

In 1777, the Shawnee chief Cornstalk was killed during a peace mission to Fort Randolph. Blackfish, another prominent Shawnee chief, pledged to remove all white settlers from Kentucky in revenge. In the face of intensified Native raiding, Kentucky's population fell to numbers lower than before the Transylvania Land Company's purchase. But Boonesborough remained strong. Life wasn't easy for Dan and the other residents because they found themselves under constant Native harassment. In one incident in March, Dan had his ankle shattered by a Native ball.

Early in 1778, Dan had bigger problems to worry about. He led a party of 30 men to the lower salt spring of the Blue Licks to hunt and make salt. He left the men to trap beaver and was captured by a Shawnee war party. They took him back to their camp, where Dan stood before 100 braves, including Blackfish

An 1851 engraving entitled "Daniel Boone and his Friends Rescuing his Daughter Jemima." The incident occurred in July 1776, and it elevated Boone's reputation as a skilled and courageous frontiersman throughout America. There were other events during the American Revolution that had Americans talking about the adventurous Kentuckian. He was captured by the Shawnee in 1778 and lived with them for three months before making a dramatic escape after learning of a planned attack on his home of Boonesborough. Boone made it back in time to lead a defense of the settlement. But it was as much Boone's attitude as his activities that endeared him to Americans. Into his mid-80s, he dreamed of going farther west.

and Captain Will. They were pleased that they had caught the great Wide Mouth, as they knew Dan. Blackfish spoke to him through an interpreter.

"Wide Mouth, we are on the way to Boonesborough. We will kill many whites and avenge the death of Cornstalk," he declared. "Are the salt-boilers your men?"

"Yes," answered Dan.

"Then they will die."

Dan knew that his men were not expecting an attack because Natives did not usually go on the warpath during the winter. And if 30 men were killed, he knew that Boonesborough could not withstand a Native attack. Dan thought quickly.

"I will persuade my men to surrender," offered Dan, "if you treat them well and promise that they will not run the gauntlet." The gauntlet was a painful ordeal in which men were clubbed and beaten by bystanders. "I'm sure that the women and children of Boonesborough will also accompany you, but they cannot travel in the snow," he added. "Wait until spring, and we will arrange a peaceful surrender."

"Yes," replied Blackfish. "But if your men do not surrender, you will die."

The Shawnee escorted Dan to the Blue Licks. He walked into the camp followed by the braves. When the men saw the Natives, they broke for their rifles.

"Don't fire!" shouted Dan. "If you do, you'll all be massacred!"

Twenty-six men surrendered. Four were not in camp, and Dan hoped they would take word to Boonesborough. The Natives held a council to decide the fate of the captives. Debate was heated, and Dan was uncertain whether his friends would be killed or spared. Hoping to sway the council, he asked for permission to speak. Blackfish agreed.

"Brothers! What I have promised you, I can much better fulfill in the spring than now. Then the weather will be warm, and the women and children can travel from Boonesborough to the Indian towns, all to live with you as one people. You have all the young men. To kill them would displease the Great Spirit, and you could then expect future success neither in hunting nor in war. If you spare them, they will make you fine warriors and excellent hunters to kill game for your squaws and children. These young men have done you no harm. They surrendered unresistingly on my assurance that such a step was the only safe one. I consented to their capitulation on the express condition that they should be made prisoners of war and treated well. Spare them, and the Great Spirit will smile upon you."

The council narrowly decided to spare the lives of the men. Dan breathed a sigh of relief, but later that day he had new cause for concern. The braves were preparing the gauntlet. Angrily, he demanded to speak with Blackfish.

"You promised not to harm my men," he declared.

"Yes, Wide Mouth. This is not for your men, but for yourself," smiled Blackfish. "You made no such bargain for yourself. You may run the gauntlet here or back at my village of Chillicothe. But you will run it."

Dan watched as the armed braves formed two parallel lines. Warriors stripped him to his breechcloth and leggings and guided him to the head of the lines. With a whack to his backside, he was off, determined not to stumble, which might well bring death from showering tomahawks and war clubs. He later described the encounter to his grandson:

I set out full speed first running so near one line that they could not do me so much damage, and when they give back, crossed over to the other side, and by that means was likely to pass through without much hurt. Still, one struck me with a blow that cut my scalp and oozed blood over my eyes, making it difficult to see. As I neared the end, a wily fellow broke the lines for the purpose of giving me a home lick. The only way

I had to avoid his intention was to run over him by springing
at him with my head bent forward, taking him full in the
breast and prostrating him flat on his back, passing over him
unhurt.

Dan's final, unexpected move brought cheers from both the
Americans and the Natives.

The next day the Native party and their captives continued
north to Chillicothe. Once there, the villagers demanded that
the others run the gauntlet, and Blackfish's pledge was forgotten. Following that ordeal, the Shawnee adopted 17 of the men.
Blackfish himself adopted Dan, suggesting the high regard in
which the Natives held him, and named him Sheltowee (Big
Turtle). In early March, Dan accompanied Blackfish to Fort
Detroit, where the Shawnee planned to sell some of the prisoners who had not been adopted. Shawnee ally and British
Governor Henry Hamilton was eager to interrogate Boone.
Dan informed him that defenses in Kentucky were weak, and
he suggested that the settlers were ready to join with the British
if pardons for fighting against King George III were forthcoming. Dan also restated his offer to return to Boonesborough
with Blackfish to ensure the surrender of the fort and to lead
the residents north into British territory. Dan was lying in order
to buy time for his men and Boonesborough.

By June, the Natives were preparing to ride to Boonesborough, while Dan was planning his escape. He had been collecting supplies and had been able to fashion a musket out
of abandoned parts. While the braves were hunting, Dan fled
and hurried to Boonesborough, where he discovered that most
of its residents were gone. Of his own family, only his daughter
Jemima remained; the others thought him dead and had
returned to North Carolina. Anticipating the Shawnee attack,
Dan urged hurried additions to the fort and sent word of the
Shawnee's plan to authorities in Virginia. But days passed and

the warriors failed to appear. Dan soon learned that Blackfish had delayed the attack until he had discussed Dan's escape with Hamilton. By August, Blackfish was ready to ride, and 450 warriors arrived at Boonesborough on September 7, 1778.

"Sheltowee!" called Blackfish. "Come out and meet with me. I have letters from Hamilton."

Dan saw the white truce flag, left the fort and approached Blackfish. The pair shook hands.

"My son, what made you leave me in the manner you did?" asked Blackfish.

"I wanted to see my wife and children so badly that I could not stay any longer," answered Dan.

"If you had let me know, I would have let you go at any time and given you my assistance. I have come with my braves so that you can deliver those in the fort to us."

Dan ignored the statement.

"You have a letter from Hamilton?" he asked.

Blackfish produced it. The message said that the people of Boonesborough would be taken back to Detroit, where they would be well treated as British subjects. Failure to surrender would result in their massacre.

"Since I have been gone, new men have been appointed commanders," said Dan. "I must speak with them."

Blackfish agreed. When Dan returned to the fort, he told the others that a fight was inevitable. Everyone knew that the odds were against Boonesborough. They were only 60 people with just 40 muskets. In an effort to convince the warriors that more people lived in Boonesborough, the women dressed in men's clothes and marched back and forth in front of the fort's gate.

Later that night, Dan met again with Blackfish.

"What is your decision?" demanded Blackfish.

"We will not go to Detroit, and we will defend the fort to the last man," replied Dan. "And I would like to thank my father for providing us extra time to strengthen the fort."

Blackfish took the decision surprisingly well.

"Then we will make treaty," he declared.

The offer was unexpected, but Dan agreed. Even as the two sides negotiated over the following days, Dan remained uncertain of Blackfish's sincerity. His suspicions proved well founded. When the treaty was signed, the Natives paired off with the settlers to shake their hands.

"Go!" Blackfish suddenly shouted.

The warriors tried to drag the settlers away from the fort. But Dan had prepared those inside it for treachery. Posted sharpshooters fired, and the men broke free during the ensuing chaos. As the men ran for the fort, warriors around the treaty grounds opened fire on them. Squire was hit, and Dan suffered a blow across the back of the head from a tomahawk. Once the Americans were back inside the fort, the Natives tried to set fire to it. When that failed, they pretended to withdraw, hoping to draw out the settlers. None came. Warriors tried to dig their way in, but heavy rain turned the earth to mud. Finally, on September 17, the Shawnee gave up in frustration. Boonesborough had lost two men; the Natives nearly 40, including the important chief Pompey.

For his efforts, Colonel Richard Callaway and Captain Benjamin Logan charged Dan with treason. Both prominent and influential leaders in Kentucky, his accusers wanted Dan stripped of his commission. They argued that Dan had given up the salt-makers to save his own life, that he had negotiated with Hamilton to give up the people at Boonesborough and that he had exposed his officers to danger by making treaty away from the protection of the fort. Callaway and Logan were also opponents of Henderson and saw the accusations against his right-hand man as a way to undermine the businessman's authority. Dan claimed that his actions and words were designed to save the fort. A court-martial was decided in Dan's favor, and he was promoted to major. Dan was vindicated, but he could not easily forget the accusations. He headed back to his family in North Carolina, where he remained for more than a year.

In the fall of 1779, Dan returned to Kentucky leading another group of settlers along the Wilderness Road. It was imperative that he return because the Transylvania Land Company's purchase had been declared invalid by authorities in Virginia. Dan needed to get to Kentucky to confirm his land claims before the Virginia land commission, which was holding hearings in the region. He established title to 1400 acres and built Boone's Station (near present-day Athens, Ohio) to the north, away from most of the new settlers. In early 1780 he headed back to Virginia with some $50,000 (some belonging to his friends) to make new land purchases. The money was stolen at an inn in James City, Virginia. Dan thought the thief was the innkeeper, but he couldn't prove it. Dan was left destitute; everything he had earned since first visiting Kentucky a decade before was gone.

Dan returned to Kentucky and his first love, hunting. It remained a dangerous activity because the Natives continued to raid, and Dan had a few close encounters. In July he joined General George Rogers Clark's expedition against the Shawnee towns of Chillicothe and Piqua. By fall he was back at Boonesborough, where more heartache waited. Natives had killed his brother Edward while he was making salt. Dan assembled a party to go in pursuit of the warriors, but didn't catch up with them.

Dan's life changed near the end of 1780, when the Virginia legislature divided Kentucky into three counties. Dan served as sheriff, deputy surveyor, lieutenant colonel of the militia and county representative to the Virginia State Assembly, a testament to the respect others continued to have for him and his abilities. But important positions didn't change Dan, who showed up for the assembly meeting in Richmond, Virginia, dressed in his comfortable buckskins. In April 1781, the assembly was forced by advancing British troops, who were part of Lord Cornwallis' southern campaign against the rebellious Americans, to relocate to Charlottesville. There Colonel Banastre Tarleton attacked them, and while most escaped, Dan was captured. Tarleton questioned him, but the colonel thought the buckskin-clad man to be inconsequential and released him in mid-June. Dan returned to Kentucky.

In 1782, frontier violence in Kentucky approached a new level of bloodiness. In August, the Natives and the British attacked the community of Bryan's Station. The residents displayed courage before the onslaught and refused to surrender. Only four were killed before the Natives retreated to the Ohio River. Dan was one of nearly 200 men who gathered at the station soon after. Despite his advice to delay until Benjamin Logan arrived with his 500 reinforcements, the men decided to pursue the fleeing warriors. Led by Colonel John Todd, they followed the Native trail to the Blue Licks. Dan was uncomfortable with what he saw. The Natives were moving slowly, and he knew that the territory provided good opportunity for an ambush. Dan expressed his concern to Todd, and as they discussed tactics, an impatient officer, concerned that delay would allow the Natives to escape, rode through camp encouraging others to follow him in an immediate attack. Many followed him. Dan described what happened next:

> The savages, observing us, gave way and we, being ignorant of their numbers, passed the [Licking] river. When the enemy saw our proceedings, having greatly the advantage of us in situation, they formed the line of battle, from one bend of Licking to the other, about a mile from the Blue Licks. An exceeding fierce battle immediately began, for about 15 minutes, when, we being overpowered by numbers, were obliged to retreat with the loss of 67 men, 7 of whom were taken prisoners.

Colonel Daniel Boone by Chester Harding, 1820; the only life
portrait of the frontiersman

One of the dead was Dan's son Israel. Only seven of the
enemy died. Although Dan wasn't responsible for the disaster,
he blamed himself for failing to convince the men to wait for
Logan.

Native raiding fell off in late 1782 as the Americans and
the British began peace talks. When the Treaty of Paris was
signed in April 1783, the British stopped supplying Natives
with weapons and supplies, and frontier violence decreased

markedly. By then Dan was enjoying great prosperity and unexpected popularity. He was living in Limestone (Maysville), Kentucky, where he operated a store and tavern. The businesses prospered as Kentucky-bound settlers floating down the Ohio River disembarked at the community. Dan was also contracted by the government to supply Native prisoners. He continued to survey, often collecting up to half the land surveyed for a claimant as payment. Perhaps some saw Dan's fee as steep, but his intimate knowledge of Kentucky, which was shared by few others, allowed him to charge what he saw fit. By the late 1780s, Dan owned more than 100,000 acres of land and three slaves. His reputation grew in 1784, when John Filson wrote the *Discovery, Settlement and Present State of Kentucke* and included an appendix on Boone's adventures. In 1789, he moved to Point Pleasant, Virginia, where pressure from the local population resulted in his appointment as lieutenant colonel of the county militia. He was a delegate at the 1791 Virginia Assembly, and he continued to expand his business enterprises by contracting with the government to supply the county's militia.

The high times of the late 1780s soon gave way to the terrible 1790s. Dan faced a series of monumental financial setbacks, most of them related to his surveying. Dan was much better at selecting good land than he was at clearing legal title to it, which was part of his responsibility. Often he failed to register claims properly, both those he made for himself and on behalf of others. The problem stemmed somewhat from legal ignorance, but it also reflected the imprecise nature of frontier surveying. Surveyors used trees and rocks as markers and so overlapping claims were inevitable. As early as 1785, Dan was facing lawsuits, and by the 1790s, he was awash in them. The legal actions were costly. Dan lost his best landholdings and saw his hard-earned reputation erode.

In 1795, Dan moved to Brushy Fork near the Blue Licks, but his frustration with the situation in Kentucky caused him to turn his eyes west. That year he had sent his son Daniel Morgan Boone into the Spanish territory of Missouri to investigate the possibility of moving there. Young Daniel returned with reports of open spaces and abundant game. Furthermore, he informed his father that Spanish authorities were eager to populate the region and would welcome Dan and anyone who accompanied him with substantial land grants. Dan hesitated at the thought of moving to a new country, but a decision by Kentucky authorities to sell 10,000 acres of his land for back taxes extinguished any lingering doubt. In September 1799, at age 64, Dan loaded all his belongings into a homemade 60-foot dugout canoe and, with family and friends, headed for Missouri.

When asked why he was leaving Kentucky, Dan replied, "Too many people! Too crowded, too crowded! I want more elbow room."

Dan reached St. Louis in October and moved into his son's house in the Femme Osage district north of the Missouri River. Spanish officials were true to their word and allowed Dan to select and portion out land grants to those accompanying him. Dan was also given his choice of 850 acres anywhere in the district, significantly more than was given to others. Soon after, Dan was busy with a new land scheme. On the banks of the Missouri he surveyed Missouriton (near present-day Augusta). Also called Daniel Boone's Palatinate, Dan hoped to attract wealthy Virginians, but the scheme fell through when much of the land was washed away by a change in the river's course.

In July 1800, the Spanish lieutenant-governor appointed Dan syndic (magistrate) of Femme Osage, endowing him with legal responsibilities that made him the most powerful man in the district. He held court near his cabin, under what became known as the "Justice Tree." Although he had no legal training, Dan heard evidence, decided guilt or innocence and handed out punishment as appropriate, usually in a direct way and with few complaints. The French took control of the territory in October 1800, and the Americans did the same in April 1803, but neither government was eager to disrupt local practices, so Dan continued with his duties for some years.

But the United States' Louisiana Purchase of 1803 did bring dramatic changes to Dan's life. A federal land commission arrived in Missouri to investigate land claims, and in 1806, they began to examine Dan's holdings. Dan discovered that he had not properly registered his claims under Spanish law, and he lost his Missouri holdings in 1809. His fortune mostly gone, Dan suffered another blow as he came to realize that the hunting he enjoyed so much didn't bring the pleasure it once did. Game abounded, but rheumatism and scrofula slowed him down. He volunteered to fight in the War of 1812, but at nearly 80, his fighting days were behind him. Still, he helped where he could as a sentry and a doctor.

In 1813, Dan's wife Rebecca died. Dan continued to explore into Kansas and along the Platte River. In 1817 he returned to Kentucky to pay off his last debts. Dan died on September 26, 1820, surrounded by family and dreaming of California and lands not yet explored.

CHAPTER TWO

Davy Crockett
1786–1836

IN MIDSUMMER A FEW YEARS AFTER the last cannon fire of the American Revolution, there occurred a significant incident, or so David (Davy) Crockett declared some years later in 1834.

> *I should not only inform the public that I was born, myself, as well as other folks, but that this important event took place, according to the best information I have received on the subject, on the 17th day of August, in the year 1786; whether by day or night, I believe I never heard, but if I did I have forgotten. I suppose however that it is not material...to the world, as the more important fact is well attested, that I was born; and, indeed, it might be inferred from my present size and appearance, that I was born pretty well.*

Davy's parents were Mary (Hawkins) from Maryland and John, an Irishman. The world was introduced to Davy at the mouth of the Limestone Creek on the Nolichucky River in Greene County, Tennessee. Like many of his time, he was one of a large family, the fifth son of nine children. Davy didn't make many memories in Greene County. His family was a rambling sort, whose relocations were sometimes the result of his father's bad business luck. By the age of eight he had moved three times, experiences that left indelible marks on Davy. In 1794, John opened a small tavern on the road from Abingdon, Virginia, to Knoxville, Tennessee. The business enjoyed a modest success, and it served as Davy's home for the remainder of his childhood.

Adventure was attracted to Davy, and when he was 12 years old, it came calling. The Crocketts had little money, and when a Dutchman stopped at the tavern in search of assistance with his large herd of cattle, John hired out his son. When the 400-mile journey was done, Davy was given $5 for his efforts.

"This, however, I think was bait for me," said Davy, "as he persuaded me to stay with him and not return to my father. I had been taught so many lessons of obedience by my father, that I at first supposed I was bound to obey this man, or at least I was afraid to openly disobey him."

So Davy agreed to stay, but secretly set his mind on returning to his family. An opportunity arose about a month later when a wagoner Davy knew arrived at the Dutchman's house. Mr. Dunn was sympathetic as Davy described his situation. He told the lad that he was staying at a tavern about seven miles distant, and that if Davy could get there early the next day, he'd get him started on the road home. Davy had a fitful night's sleep and rose well before dawn, only to find that a blizzard had blown in! The snow was eight inches deep, when Davy slipped from the house. He had to guess the route, and he knew there'd be no turning back because his footsteps were quickly filled in by the heavy snowfall. He took some comfort in knowing that the old Dutchman wouldn't be able to follow him. When he stumbled into the tavern a few hours later, the snow was knee deep. Davy was warmed by the fire and given some breakfast before the Dunn party set out.

Davy soon tired of the slow pace of the wagons and decided to hurry ahead on foot. It was a most natural way of traveling for Davy, who had already spent long, happy hours wandering through the woods with his musket.

"Mr. Dunn seemed very sorry to part with me and used many arguments to prevent me from leaving him," said Davy. "But home, poor as it was, again rushed on my memory, and it seemed 10 times as dear to me as it had ever before. The reason was, that my parents were there and all that I had been accustomed to in the hours of childhood and infancy was there."

Davy left Dunn and eventually fell in with a kindly stranger who offered him the use of a spare horse. Soon he was home, where he admitted, his "anxious heart panted to be."

But Davy didn't remain there long. The following spring his father sent him to a nearby one-room school, attended by students of various ages, sizes and abilities. Davy wasn't in school a week before he got into a scrap with an older boy named Kitchen. Davy whupped the boy, but refused to return to the school for fear he'd receive a licking from the schoolmaster as punishment. Davy might have done better to worry about his father's anger. When John discovered his son's truancy, he found a switch of green hickory and promised to put it to good use on Davy's behind if he didn't get to school. John emphasized his point by chasing his son in the direction of the school. But Davy was fleet of foot and obstinate. He slipped into the woods, and once beyond his father's reach, made for the house of a neighbor, whom Davy knew was preparing to drive cattle to Virginia. Soon Davy was headed east, eventually reaching Front Royal some 400 miles distant. When the cattle were sold, Davy was left with $4 pay and no job. It was no great problem as Davy discovered; in 1799 a willing young man found work easily. But it was not easy to forget about home.

"I often thought of home," admitted Davy, "and, indeed, wished bad enough to be there; but, when I thought of the schoolhouse and Kitchen, my master and the race with my father, and the big hickory he carried, and of the fierceness of the storm of wrath that I had left him in, I was afraid to venture back; for I knew my father's nature so well that I was certain his anger would hang on to him like a turtle does to a fisherman's toe, and that, if I went back in a hurry, he would give me the devil in three or four ways."

Instead, Davy went to Baltimore, where he found himself attracted to the harbor front. He thought about signing on with a London-bound ship, but ultimately headed west. He wandered home in the spring of 1802, where he discovered the heated passions he so worried about had long since cooled. Davy found his father deep in debt, so he went to work for a neighbor to help the family's financial situation. Davy didn't quit until he was able to give his father a fistful of money.

Davy finally moved out of his parents' home in August 1806, when he married Polly Finlay. They built a house in Weakley County, Tennessee, and had two sons within a few years. But Davy found making a living there to be a losing proposition, so he set his sights on newly opened territory in southern Tennessee. In the fall of 1811, the Crocketts moved to the head of the Mulberry Fork of the Elk River in Lincoln County. Davy was most pleased by the abundance of game, and he soon gained a reputation as a hunter. Folks began calling him "Dead-shot" and considered any shooting contest he entered already won. But Davy loved bear hunting above all else, and unfortunately, few bears could be found in Lincoln County. Perhaps that was why he moved on to Bean Creek, near Winchester, in 1812.

Davy didn't have much of a chance to scout the local bear population. In June, the United States, tired of British harassment of its ships in the Atlantic and land hungry for British territory beyond the Ohio Valley, declared war on Great Britain.

Mezzotint of Colonel David Crockett by C.G. Stuart, 1839, from a portrait by John Gadsby Chapman, 1834

The declaration brought immediate problems to the frontier. Many Natives saw war as an opportunity to halt American expansion westward. Around Davy's home, the Creek were among the most formidable of the Natives, and in 1813, the Red Stick faction of that tribe went on the warpath in what was known as the Creek War. Among their first targets was Fort Mims on the Alabama River. In August, Chief William

Weatherford led 800 warriors on that poorly defended position, resulting in the death of over 400 soldiers and settlers.

When Davy heard of the violent attack on Fort Mims, his
blood ran hot. "I instantly felt like going," he acknowledged,
"and I had none of the dread of dying that I expected to feel."
When he heard that authorities were mustering a militia at
nearby Winchester, he informed his wife that he was going to
do his duty.

"Davy, please don't turn out," begged Polly. "I'm a stranger
in these parts, and if you go, you'll leave the children and me in
a lonesome and unhappy situation."

"My countrymen have been murdered," Davy reminded
her, "and the Indians won't stop with them. Soon they'll be
scalping women and children unless we put a stop to it."

Polly turned from her husband, and he placed his hand on
her shoulder.

"If every man waits until his wife gets willing for him to go
to war, there'll be no fighting done and we'll all die in our
houses."

She was crying as Davy put an end to the discussion, "I'm as
able to go as any man, and I've got a duty to my country."

Davy went to Winchester and enlisted for a 90-day tour of
duty. He was detailed to Alabama with 1300 volunteers. While
his company was camped at Beaty's Spring, south of Huntsville,
Major John Gibson arrived in search of woodsmen to accompany him on a reconnaissance into Creek territory. Davy was
singled out as the best among the volunteers. Early the next
morning, the 13-man party forded the Tennessee River. The
party divided with Davy in charge of five men. They eventually
found a small camp of friendly Creek. Davy and his men set
up camp nearby and joined the Natives in some shooting con-
tests. The Creek enjoyed the competition but were worried.

"If the Red Sticks come and find you here, all of us will be
killed," the chief informed Davy.

"I'll keep watch tonight," replied Davy, "and if one shows up, I'll carry the skin of his head home to make me a moccasin."

Everyone laughed at this welcome show of bravado, but when Davy turned in that night he cradled his rifle. He was wakened by what he called "the sharpest scream that ever escaped the throat of a human creature." He soon learned that it came from a recently arrived Native who brought news of the approach of a large war party of Red Stick Creek warriors. Davy realized that he had to get back to the militia's base camp to inform his superiors. His men rode hard to cover the 65 miles, but Davy was in for a surprise when he arrived and relayed the information to Colonel John Coffee, commanding officer of the troops near Huntsville.

"He didn't seem to mind my report a bit," seethed Davy, "and this raised my dander higher than ever; but I knowed that I had to be on my best behavior, and so I kept it all to myself; though I was so mad that I was burning inside like a tarkiln, and I wonder that the smoke hadn't been pouring out of me at all points."

Coffee doubted the accuracy of Crockett's information because he believed it was the fanciful imagining of an inexperienced soldier. But when Major Gibson returned the next day with similar intelligence, Coffee ordered the construction of breastworks. He also sent word to Andrew Jackson, major general of the Tennessee volunteers at Nashville, to get his troops marching before the Creek wiped out the militia. Jackson's men arrived by the second week of October. In early November the Red Stick Creek were finally engaged at the Battle of Talishatchee. Fueled by memories of the attack on Fort Mims, the men fought with wild abandon, as Davy described, "we shot them like dogs." The Creek lost almost 200 warriors, while only five soldiers were killed.

A few weeks later Davy served under General Jackson at the Battle of Talledega, which resulted in the convincing defeat of

Chief William Weatherford. After the battle, many of the volunteers told Jackson of their desire to return home. The weather was cooling, provisions were scarce, horses were in bad shape, and for the most part, their term of enlistment was up. Davy still had a few weeks to serve, but he was also anxious to get back to his family. Jackson thought of future battles and denied the requests. To underline his position, he trained cannon on the bridge that led north to the men's homes. Davy bristled at Jackson's high-handedness and encouraged the volunteers to leave anyway. Many took his lead.

"We got ready and moved on till we came near the bridge, where the general's men were all strung along on both sides," described Davy. "But we all had our flints ready picked and guns ready primed, that if we were fired on we might fight our way through, or all die together. When we came still nearer the bridge we heard the guards cocking their guns, and we did the same. But, after all, we marched boldly on, and not a gun was fired, nor a life lost."

While Davy was eager to return home, he wasn't of a mind to quit the militia. After he had rested up and re-supplied, he re-enlisted for another six-month term. He saw action at the Battle of Enitachopco in late January 1814, but other encounters were small and scattered. Before spring arrived, Davy was on furlough and back home.

"I began to feel as though I had done Indian fighting enough for one time," he explained.

Davy still wanted a chance to fight the British, and in the spring of 1814, he again volunteered and marched to Pensacola, Florida. By the time Davy's company had woven its way south in November, General Jackson had already secured the town, and a disappointed Davy was forced to watch the departing British ships. Davy then headed back north with 1000 other volunteers. For a time his backwoods expertise was put to use as a scout and hunter in Native country. They had a few encounters with the Creek, but they were mostly a defeated enemy after the Battle of Horseshoe Bend in March 1814 (they finally made treaty in August). More troubling was the lack of provisions. The men were often without food for days, and hunting skills were of little value when no game could be found. Davy told one story that describes the trials faced by the men.

> I found a squirrel; which I shot, but he got into a hole in the tree. The game was small, but necessity is not very particular; so I thought I must have him, and I climbed that tree 30 feet high, without a limb, and pulled him out of his hole. I shouldn't relate such small matters only to show what lengths a hungry man will go to, to get something to eat.

Davy returned home a lieutenant in early 1815 with his desire for soldiering spent. His wife died soon after, leaving Davy with two boys and an infant girl. Davy wanted his children to have a mother, so he quickly remarried a war widow, Elizabeth Patton, who had two children of her own. Davy enjoyed the better part of two years at home with his family but eventually felt the need to return to the trail. In the fall of 1816, he set out with a few neighbors to explore the newly opened Creek country. They wound their way as far southwest as present-day Tuscaloosa, Alabama, despite suffering problems on their journey. While camped one evening, a horse got away. Davy gave chase, some 50 miles he reckoned, across creeks, through swamps and over hills. He never did catch the horse, but he did catch a bad case of malaria. Only the arrival of some friendly Natives, who took him to a nearby house, and the limited doctoring skills of the people who lived there, helped Davy recover, but he was troubled by recurring bouts of fever for the rest of his life.

Davy returned home to his astonished wife. His traveling companions had assured her that Davy was dead and buried.

Davy took his family and moved on. They spent some time in southern Kentucky, but in the spring of 1817, set up house at the head of Shoal Creek in present-day Lawrence County, Tennessee. He built a small log house, a gristmill, a powder mill and a distillery. The costly enterprises put Davy in debt, but he was soon making money because the population of Lincoln County was booming. Unfortunately, not all the newcomers were honest farmers. The locals were soon troubled by the arrival of a lawless element, and in the tradition of frontier living, folks took it upon themselves to deal with the problem. They established a local government.

"We met and appointed magistrates and constables to keep order," said Davy. "We didn't fix any laws for them, though; for we supposed that they would know law enough, whoever they might be, and so we left it to themselves to fix the laws."

Representatives appointed Davy as one of the magistrates, and in November 1817, the appointment was made official by the state legislature. Davy issued warrants, judged the accused and assigned sentences ranging from fines to whippings. The writing demanded by the position was a challenge for Davy, and although he was ignorant of the finer points of the law, he was proud that none of his decisions were ever overturned. He served as a magistrate until November 1819.

While fulfilling his civic duty, Crockett was approached by Captain Matthews of the local militia with a surprising proposal. In these days, officers of county militia regiments were elected. Matthews was running for the colonelcy of the regiment, and he asked Davy to put his name forward for the office of major in an effort to gain the frontiersman's support. Davy reluctantly agreed, only to discover later that Matthews' son was running for the same office! Davy confronted the captain about his underhanded conniving.

"It's true, Crockett," stated Matthews. "My son is a candidate. But he hates worse to run against you than any man in the county."

"Well, captain," replied Davy, "your son need give himself no uneasiness about that because I won't be running against him for major. I'll be running against his daddy for colonel."

Davy later explained that since he had to take on the whole family, he might as well "levy on the head of the mess."

Davy won the election and was commissioned lieutenant colonel commandant of the 57th Regiment of the Militia in March 1818. It wasn't long after that friends approached him to run as representative for Lawrence and Hickman counties in the state legislature. Again Davy agreed with some hesitation. He had learned something about politicking in his run for the colonelcy. It required speeches, and Davy was uncomfortable about giving them. But he was a quick study, and it wasn't long before he had figured out something of the politician's art, as he related after he first visited Hickman County.

"Here they told me that they wanted to move their town nearer to the center of the county, and I must come out in favor of it." They meant that they wanted the county seat moved closer to their town, but Davy was confused. "There's no devil in me if I knowed what this meant, or how the town was to be moved; and so I kept dark, going on the plan…called 'noncommittal.' "

Then he joined in a squirrel hunt, something he knew plenty about. The men were divided into two parties, and the side bringing in the fewest tails paid for the barbecue. Davy shot plenty of squirrels and brought his side victory.

Eventually, it was time for the speeches. Davy agreed to let his opponent speak first. He found this to be a good strategy because folks were so tired of listening by his turn that he rarely had to say much. It also allowed him to bone up on his knowledge of government and politics by noting the points his opponent made.

"I reckon you know what I come for," said Davy, when he took the stump, "but if not, I can tell you. I've come for your votes, and if you don't watch mighty close, I'll get them too!"

But Davy made a mistake when he turned to the subject of government. Still a neophyte, he couldn't tell them anything about a subject he knew little about.

"I choked up as bad as if my mouth had been jam'd and cram'd chock full of dry mush," he later admitted.

"I'm like a fellow I heard of not long ago," he confessed to the crowd. "He was beating on the head of an empty barrel near the roadside, when a traveler who was passing along, asked him what he was doing that for? The fellow replied that there was some cider in the barrel a few days before, and he was trying to see if there was any left, but if there was, he could not get at it. There was a little bit of speech in me a while ago, but I don't believe I can get it out!"

The crowd laughed at this, and Davy continued on with some other funny stories. He had found the campaigning strategy he would use for years to come.

"I thank you for your attention," he concluded. "But now my mouth's as dry as a powder horn. I think it's time we all wet our whistles."

Davy headed for the liquor stand, followed by most of the crowd, whom he kept entertained with stories between horns of whiskey. On Election Day, Davy's votes more than doubled his competitor's. Davy entered the legislature in 1821, but he soon had more troubles than politics. His mills flooded, and with no grain, he had to close his distillery, surely a crushing blow for a fellow as fond of whiskey as Davy. In later years, he was able to joke about the matter, suggesting "that the misfortune just made a complete mash of me." His losses were a considerable—$3000—but with the support of his wife, Davy made good on his debts by selling his property and moving on.

Davy made a new start of it when the legislative session ended. He scouted a region 150 miles northwest near the Obion River in Carroll County, Tennessee. He found that he liked the hunting there and put in a crop. When he built a log house, his family joined him. Life was challenging on the Obion, where the closest neighbor was miles away. The winter of 1822 found the Crocketts without powder, a serious matter for people who depended on hunting for survival. Davy decided to set out for his brother-in-law's, six miles away. His wife objected; it was cold, and the river to be crossed was at least a mile wide and running high. Davy ignored her concerns; the powder was needed.

When he left his house, the snow was four inches deep. He broke trail to the river a quarter of a mile away and trembled when he saw the breadth of the swollen river. The sandbars he had often used to ford the river were mostly submerged, making the far side appear fearfully distant. Davy found some jammed logs and carefully made his way along them. His luck ran out when one of the logs turned over in deep water. Although he dropped down to his chin, he had the presence of mind to keep his rifle and a pack of fresh clothes above water. He waded out and changed his clothes, but the chill from the icy water had seeped into his bones. His condition was perilous, and Davy knew that he had to warm up. He tried to run, but the cold had shortened his stride to a shuffle. It was in that stiff, painful state that he stumbled into his brother-in-law's home that evening.

The next day the temperature fell, and his brother-in-law persuaded Davy to remain for a few days. But Davy was worried about his family so he didn't stay long. When he returned to the river, he saw that it had a thin crust of ice over all but the fast flowing middle. The ice wouldn't support his weight, so he was forced to wade through the freezing water, having to make a couple of trips to get both the powder and his gun across. He arrived home to find his wife certain that he was dead.

"It was a close call," Davy told her. "I didn't know how much any body could suffer and not die."

Davy was still concerned about bringing in some meat, and he was excited when his brother-in-law and a friend arrived to invite him hunting. They informed Davy that the river was now frozen.

"We're going down to the river to shoot turkeys," said one.

"To heck with the gobblers," said Davy. "I'll be after bigger game. I dreamed last night that I had a hard fight with a big blackie, and I know it was a sign that I'm to have a battle with bear. Never knowed such a dream to fail in bear country," he added.

Davy called his dogs and headed down along the river. Several hours later his dogs had scared up nothing but a couple of turkeys. The weather turned, and a miserable sleet fell. Adding to his frustration was the strange behavior of his dogs. They barked at the base of trees, where Davy could find no game. Davy's anger grew, and he was ready to shoot the oldest of the hounds when he came to a meadow and saw "the biggest bear that was ever seen in America." The dogs, he realized suddenly, hadn't been off. They just didn't want to reach the bear before their master. Davy chuckled; he loved nothing more than a bear hunt, and here was a real challenge.

The dogs set on the bear and treed it. Davy crawled to within 80 yards of the animal and fired on it. The bear waved his paw as if it was knocking the shot away. When Davy shot another round, the bear fell from the tree. The animal crashed to the ground and grabbed a dog, which howled in protest.

"I took my tomahawk in one hand and my big butcher knife in the other, and ran up within four or five paces of him," said Davy, "at which he let my dog go and fixed his eyes on me. I got back in all sorts of a hurry, for I knowed if he got hold of me, he would hug me altogether too close for comfort. I went to my gun and hastily loaded her again and shot him the third time, which killed him good."

Davy was quite pleased and not just because the bear weighed 600 pounds.

"I now felt fully compensated for my sufferings in going after my powder and well satisfied that a dog might sometimes be doing a good business even when he seemed to be *barking up the wrong tree.*"

The closest town to Davy's new home was Jackson. He went there to sell furs and to buy supplies, so the locals knew him. Perhaps they also knew something of his background because in 1823, they insisted that he run for the state legislature. Davy allowed himself to be convinced, and despite a good number of candidates, he was elected. During this term in office, Davy demonstrated something of his independent streak. The term of the local senator Colonel John Williams had expired, and his opponents figured that their man, General Andrew Jackson, could defeat the incumbent in the upcoming election. Jackson was in nomination for the presidency, but agreed to put his name forward. The majority in the legislature voted for Jackson, but Crockett was not among them.

"I thought the colonel had honestly discharged his duty," said Davy in defense of his vote, "and even the mighty name of Jackson couldn't make me vote against him. I supported the public interest and cleared my conscience in giving it, instead of gratifying the private ambition of a man."

The voters liked what they heard and re-elected Davy in 1825. He did, however, lose his run for Congress later that year. But Davy kept busy, mainly hunting bear. To better his odds, he increased his dogs from three to eight, all as fierce as panthers. Davy hunted down towards the Mississippi River and in the territory between Obion and Reelfoot lakes. By his account, he killed 47 bears in less than one month and 105 throughout

1825–26! A good portion of the meat went to friends and neighbors, some of whom sought Davy out so that they might shoot with the legendary hunter. Occasionally, he invited someone who was down on his luck to join him on the hunt so that hungry families could have their bellies filled.

Davy enjoyed many adventures during that year and had many tales that he often told to willing listeners. One episode in January 1826 reveals much about the hunt and the man. Davy's dogs were in a barking frenzy, and he left his hunting partners to go in search of them. It took some time to find the animals because night had fallen, but he finally discovered them at the base of a forked poplar. Davy looked up to see a dark shape in the tree. He thought of lighting a fire to improve his vision, but could find no dry brush. So Davy decided to shoot at it. After two cracks, the bear fell, and all hell broke loose.

The bear landed among the dogs, and the crazed animals howled and growled as they rolled in a tangled knot. Davy's dogs were ferocious, but the bear held its own. As the blood of the fighting animals splattered on Davy's buckskin clothes, he unsheathed his big butcher knife for protection in case the bear broke free. He gave a grunt of satisfaction when the dogs finally holed the bear in a crack in the ground. Davy poked the muzzle of his gun in and fired. The bear roared, and Davy figured that the shot had only made it angrier. He searched for a stick while the dogs took turns jumping into the crack to torment the bear. As he returned to the crack, Davy could hear his dogs' pained yelping. This bear was giving no quarter! But that didn't deter Davy, who began to poke the bear with the stick.

Eventually, the bear's roars gave way to a low, steady growl, and Davy decided that the animal was quiet enough for him to ease into the crack to try and stab it with his butcher knife. He hollered at his dogs to get in before him to keep the bear busy. Then Davy crawled in and, careful to avoid the claws of the bear's kicking feet, placed his hand on its rump and slid it up to the animal's shoulder. Wasting no time, he plunged his knife into the bear's heart, killing it instantly.

Davy backed out of the crack and called his dogs off. He struggled to get the heavy bear out of the hole, and once he did, he butchered it. The work done, Davy was exhausted. But sleep wouldn't come because it was too cold. He tried unsuccessfully to light a fire, and it was then that Davy suddenly realized the danger of his situation. If he couldn't warm himself up, he'd freeze. He stood up and, tired as he was, began jumping and dancing and shouting, but that just made him feel even colder. He was getting desperate, when an idea came to him. He spotted an odd-looking tree that had no branches for at least 30 feet off the ground. On stiff limbs, Davy staggered to the tree, climbed up to the branches, wrapped his arms and legs tight around its trunk and slid down to the bottom. The friction warmed him up, and he repeated the action until daylight, at least 100 times, he reckoned. In the morning, he hung his bear and returned to his friends' camp. They were almost ready to give him up for lost.

Davy also engaged in lumber speculation around this time. He planned to build boats, cut staves as cargo and sail the lot down the Mississippi for sale in New Orleans. When a boat sank, and Davy nearly drowned, he returned his attention to a more familiar and safer enterprise. In August 1827, the congressional seat for western Tennessee was up for election, and Davy threw his cap into the ring. Witty stories and free whiskey did much to ingratiate the voters, who saw Davy as one of their own. And it didn't hurt that he was, at the time, a supporter of the popular Tennessee politician Andrew Jackson, whom he believed shared his concerns for the rights of squatters in his district.

Davy was elected and became something of a curiosity in Washington when he arrived there to take his seat. Unabashedly dressed in buckskins and informal in manner and speech, Davy stood out. Political opponents portrayed him as a country bumpkin, but the criticisms served to endear him to many who didn't mind hearing a politician speak frankly and in words the common man understood. People were soon arriving from outside the Capitol to see and hear him. Popularity, however, wasn't enough to save Crockett from the wrath of Jackson.

In late 1828, Davy tried to introduce a bill that protected the interests of West Tennessee squatters, but President Jackson and his followers did not support it. As part of the political intrigue that surrounded Davy's proposal, Jackson's supporters tried to have him defeated in the election of 1829. But Davy's popularity was great, and he was re-elected with an even greater majority than in 1827. Davy felt he knew something of the real Jackson by this time, and he wasn't happy about the revelation.

"I saw, or thought I did, that it was expected of me to bow to the name of Andrew Jackson and follow him in all his motions, and mindings, and turnings, even at the expense of my conscience and judgment," observed Davy. "Such a thing was new to me and a total stranger to my principles."

Davy's revelation was accurate. Jackson was known to turn on even loyal supporters if they voiced a difference of opinion. And Davy was a major dissenting voice in 1830, when Jackson introduced legislation designed to clear the frontier of Natives so that it might be opened for settlement. While the Indian Removal Act passed, Crockett argued for Native rights and cast the only Tennessee vote against it. Davy returned home to a hornets' nest. Everyone knew that he had committed the "unpardonable sin" of turning against Jackson.

"I was hunted down like a wild varmint," said Davy, "and in this hunt every little paper in the district and every little pinhook lawyer was engaged."

Davy was defeated in the 1831 election. But the loss only increased his determination, and despite the continued active opposition of Jackson's supporters, Davy was re-elected in

1833. He considered it a great moral victory, one that allowed him "to vote as my conscience and judgment dictates to be right, without the yoke of any party on me or the driver at my heels, with his whip in hand, commanding me to ge-wo-haw just at his pleasure. Look at my neck," declared Davy, "you will not find there any collar, with the engraving, 'MY DOG. ANDREW JACKSON.' "

His independent streak, which he trumpeted in his motto, "Be always sure you're right—then go ahead," sometimes raised eyebrows. Such was the case when he stood in Congress and made a speech against donating public money to the widow of a distinguished naval officer. Fellow members were shocked at the lone voice of opposition. Davy explained his position on constitutional grounds. It was his opinion, formed as a result of a conversation he'd had with a thoughtful elector, that the measure overstepped the legal boundaries of Congress.

"We have the right, as individuals, to give away as much of our own money as we please in charity," said Davy to the Speaker, "but as members of Congress, we have no right so to appropriate a dollar of the public money."

In concluding his speech, Davy noted, "I am the poorest man on this floor. I cannot vote for this bill, but I will give one week's pay to the object, and if every member of Congress will do the same, it will amount to no more than the bill asks."

The bill passed and congressional pockets were not lightened.

In 1834, Davy's star was at its zenith. Biographies were published, and his almanacs, with hunting tips and personal anecdotes added to the traditional fare of agricultural and weather information, were bestsellers. He also published his autobiography that year, and Davy discovered something of his popularity on a spring and summer tour of the northeast. From Baltimore to Boston and Philadelphia to Pittsburgh, folks came to hear him and "to shake hands with an honest man."

The Young Whigs even gave him a fancy new rifle, although it's hard to imagine it ever replaced Old Betsy.

But national popularity did not win him re-election in 1835. The forces of Jackson were against him, and in Jackson's home state of Tennessee, these were formidable forces indeed. The good stories, the twists of tobacco, the horns of whiskey weren't enough for victory this time.

When he was defeated, Davy declared, "The constituents can go to hell, and I'll go to Texas!"

For many Americans, Texas was a land of opportunity and adventure, a place where the hopeful and determined could make a fresh start. Since Mexico had won its independence from Spain in 1821, the government had encouraged American immigration, and many had settled in the territory north of the Rio Grande. While their rights were protected by the Mexican constitution of 1824, Mexican authorities were concerned about the growing power of the Americans in Texas and the close relations they maintained with their homeland. By 1830, the property and self-governance rights of American Texans were under attack. And in 1835, Antonio López de Santa Anna, the president of Mexico, overthrew the constitution and proclaimed himself dictator of Mexico. He proclaimed martial law and set about disarming the Texans. They resisted, and war began in October.

Davy liked what he heard about Texas. He wasn't too concerned about Texan independence, but he realized that if he was to homestead and perhaps run for office there, Texas would have to throw off the yoke of Santa Anna. He was headed south by November 1835 and passed many empty cabins throughout Arkansas, most of their owners having already made the same decision to head to Texas. Still, whenever he came to a town, locals pressed him to make a speech; such was his continuing popularity. Davy was particularly taken by the Red River valley in southwestern Arkansas and thought about

With a flourish, Crockett inscribed below his portrait, "I have this rule, for others when I am dead—be always sure you are right, then go ahead." Perhaps it was this principled and stubborn philosophy that led Crockett to Texas after losing the 1835 congressional election. Eventually, Crockett made his way to San Antonio, where he joined Jim Bowie and 180 other Texans set on independence from Mexico. While the rebels were defeated by Santa Anna's superior forces in March 1836, news of their valiant but doomed defense of the Alamo traveled north, and they became heroes in the eyes of many Americans. Crockett, one of the last surviving holdouts, soon became a legend.

settling there. But Davy heard about an upcoming provisional government and Constitutional Convention in San Antonio and sensed a political opportunity. He took the Texas oath of allegiance, which gave him entry into the political life of the community, and made for San Antonio. Davy arrived in the city to find a political debate brewing between Sam Houston, commander in chief of the Texan forces and a supporter of Jackson, and a more conservative element called the General Council that planned both the provisional government and the Constitutional Convention. Davy fell in with the latter group. Many of the officers who supported the General Council were stationed at the Alamo, a 60-year-old garrison that was originally a Spanish mission and then a fort in the center of San Antonio. Davy made his way there.

Davy was still at the Alamo when Santa Anna and his 5000 troops arrived in San Antonio in February 1836. Santa Anna was determined to avenge a Mexican defeat suffered there in December and to put an end to the locals' thoughts of independence. On February 23, he laid siege to the Alamo and the 187 men inside. Crockett and the others, including James Bowie and William Travis, held out until early March, taking the lives of as many as 1600 Mexicans. But the Texans' fate was sealed. Santa Anna breached the Alamo's walls on March 6. Inside he found six Texans alive, including Davy. Santa Anna ordered them all executed.

CHAPTER THREE

Jim Bridger
1804–1881

ON ST. PATRICK'S DAY IN 1804, James Bridger was tapping a keg of beer when word came that his wife had given birth. Bridger, a surveyor by trade and a barkeeper by circumstance, looked around. He decided that he could be generous with the half dozen men bending elbows in his establishment, called for a round on the house and hurried upstairs to see his wife and new son. Chloe Tyler Bridger, a barmaid in his tavern, rested on a hard straw bed with her infant in her arms. They named the boy James Junior (Jim herein).

The tavern failed, and the family left Richmond, Virginia, and moved north to a farm in nearby Fredericksburg. They had no better luck there. Eventually, the Bridgers, with two sons and a daughter, turned their backs on Virginia and headed west to wide-open spaces, where Bridger anticipated a demand for his surveying skills. Jim was eight when they arrived in St. Louis, a growing town of about 1500. After making inquiries, his father purchased a farm at Six-Mile Prairie, up and across the Mississippi River from St. Louis. Bridger was soon busy surveying, so the responsibilities of the farm fell on Chloe and the children.

Young Jim didn't have much time for leisure, but when he did, he could be found on the shores of the Mississippi watching the river men, their vessels loaded with stacks of pelts and robes or crates of supplies. He listened to the men curse the work of pulling towlines that was necessary to maneuver the keelboats upriver and to the songs the French Canadian *voyageurs* sang to keep time to their dipping oars. He often wondered about their origins and destinations, but his wonderings were always short-lived because his farm chores inevitably pulled him back to reality.

In 1816, Jim's mother died, adding heartbreak to the physical demands of farming. A year later his father and brother also died. But for a few glorious months, Jim worked on a ferry that operated between Six-Mile Point and St. Louis. Jim enjoyed the company of the river men, despite work that challenged even the strongest. Jim's future, however, did not lie along the Mississippi. His aunt, who had taken charge of the farm following his mother's death, apprenticed him to a St. Louis blacksmith. For five years, Jim toiled to the rhythm of hammer and anvil in a dark forge. Fortunately, he discovered that life in St. Louis had its consolations. Jim was in regular contact with river men, traders and trappers, and he was a willing audience to any of them who might spin a tale about life in the distant west.

In early 1822 Jim heard of an advertisement placed in the local *Missouri Republican*. A pair of one-time Missouri militia officers, General William Ashley, lieutenant-governor of the state, and Major Andrew Henry, an experienced trapper, were seeking "enterprising young men" who wished "to ascend the Missouri River to its source, there to be employed for one, two, or three years." It was the opportunity Jim had long desired. He discarded his hammer and grimy overalls and scrawled his "X" on a contract with Ashley and Henry, agreeing to trap beaver on half-shares. It's possible that he fled his indentured service, although he didn't keep his intentions secret. Both his aunt and sister waved goodbye as he left St. Louis on April 15, 1822.

As they traveled up the Missouri River Jim noticed a dwindling white presence. Before summer's arrival, the military post of Fort Atkinson at the mouth of the Platte River, and the Missouri Fur Company's Fort Recovery at the mouth of the White River, were both long downstream. The rest of the journey took the expedition through Native country, and as that news filtered throughout the party, the number of desertions increased. Jim thought their flight odd. He had seen Natives in St. Louis and thought they were more to be pitied than feared, but he was in for a surprise when he finally saw the Natives unaffected by white vices in their own environment.

Jim first suspected that the Natives might be a force to be reckoned with when the expedition came upon an Arikara (Ree) village in July. Major Henry ordered that the village be approached cautiously, with rifles loaded. The Ree were as likely to shoot as trade, and Major Henry didn't want to take any chances. The Natives were in a good mood on this occasion, and Jim took some trinkets on credit from his employers and traded for a buckskin outfit. Relations were less amiable one month later, when the party happened upon a band of Assiniboine along the big bend of the Missouri River. The Natives indicated that they wanted to trade, but at the first opportunity, they stole the trapper's entire herd of 50 horses.

In mid-August the party reached its destination just above the mouth of the Yellowstone River. Major Henry supervised the building of Fort Henry, while Ashley retraced the 1800 miles to St. Louis for additional supplies and men. Jim remained, and when the fort was completed a month later, he joined a party sent out to trap beaver. With a reassuring slap on his back and advice not to go under—the phrase for dying on the job—Jim set out with his six traps. He learned quickly that trapping was demanding work. The traps were five pounds apiece, each with five feet of chain, and they had to be set mid-stream in cold creeks. Often a trapper had to walk hundreds of feet in a river so that his scent could not be detected on the shore near where he set his trap. And before he could return to the relative comfort of camp, he had to clean the trapped beaver. By mid-October, the fall trapping was completed, and Major Henry, learning of Jim's training as a smithy, put him to work in the forge that Ashley had brought with him when he had returned earlier in the month. Jim cursed his luck. Men were being sent farther west to establish an advance post, and he longed to go with them. Yet, he was stuck at Fort Henry doing what he thought he'd escaped.

Jim learned something of the dangers of trapping in 1823. First, came the news that Blackfoot warriors had killed four Henry-Ashley men above the Great Falls. Then Jedidiah Smith, who had also signed on with Ashley and Henry in Spring 1822, stumbled into Fort Henry in early June with news of trouble on the Missouri River. Smith was traveling north from St. Louis with Ashley, when Ree warriors attacked the party and killed seven men. Like the Blackfoot, the Ree were angered by the possibility that the trappers would usurp their role as middle-men in the trade with western and northern Native bands. Jim listened as Smith described how the Ree had attacked unexpectedly after they had traded with the trappers. He was in awe as Smith coolly related his own role in the fight and his subsequent willingness to hike to Fort Henry for reinforcements. Even though Smith was young, Jim could see that his counterpart had the "hair of the bear," the highest praise one mountain man could give another.

Jim joined the party that set out the next morning to assist the Ashley party, which was camped downstream from the Ree villages. They arrived in early July and discovered that Ashley had also sent word to Fort Atkinson for reinforcements. He did not want to attack the Ree until the soldiers joined the trappers.

The blue coats arrived in late July. Following a short and inde-cisive battle, the two groups made treaty. Major Henry, how-ever, remained suspicious of the Ree and feared that they would resume their aggressive ways once the soldiers departed. As a precaution, he closed Fort Henry and moved most of his trappers up the Yellowstone River into Crow country. Jim, who thought he was chained to the anvil, was excited to learn that he would be going with them.

Along the Yellowstone River a grizzled old trapper named Hugh Glass stumbled upon a bear and her two cubs. He was mauled terribly before he killed the bear, and everyone thought his death was inevitable. When Major Henry learned of the incident, he called for volunteers to remain with Glass so that he might be buried properly when the time came. The men remained quiet. No one wanted to be left alone in Native territory, and even a week with Glass meant lost wages. Per-haps in an effort to bring some attention to himself, Jim vol-unteered.

"How old are you, Bridger?" barked the major.

"Nineteen," he replied.

"I got a boy who's willing to stay. Any of you man enough to join him?" challenged Henry.

Eventually, when Major Henry promised compensation for lost wages, John Fitzgerald agreed to join Jim. But the pair was hardly alone with Glass a day before Fitzgerald suggested they should leave him.

"He's gonna die anyway. No sense in us joining him, and that's just what'll happen if the Injuns find us," suggested Fitzgerald. "And if you think that grizzly hurt Glass, wait'll you see what the Injuns have in store for us. They'll roast us alive and laugh while doing it."

"We can't just leave him here to die alone," protested Jim.

"He's as good as dead."

"Don't talk like that. He might hear us."

"He's got more to worry about than what we got to say."

Fitzgerald agreed to remain, and five days later, they were still there waiting for the old man to die.

"By God, he's tougher than an old bull buffalo," moaned Fitzgerald. "We're going, Jim. Get his rifle and knife."

"We can't take his weapons," objected Jim.

"What use is he gonna make of them? 'Sides, Henry'll know something is up if we say we buried his rifle with him. Let's go."

"But he's still alive."

"Kill him if you want. But don't use a rifle. Don't want the noise to bring the Injuns down on us."

Jim stole a final look at Glass. He didn't doubt that Glass would soon be dead, but he wasn't going to be the one to kill him. He turned away and followed Fitzgerald. When they reached Fort Henry, and Fitzgerald reported that they'd buried Glass, Jim remained silent. They learned that the party had done some trading with the Crow and that Major Henry had decided to build a new post in Crow territory. New Fort Henry, at the mouth of the Bighorn River, was completed in late 1823. And before the end of the year, the post received an unexpected guest—Hugh Glass.

Incredibly, soon after Bridger and Fitzgerald left, Glass had recovered enough of his strength to crawl east. He was driven by a single-minded determination to exact revenge on the men who had deserted him. In October, he stumbled into the French Fur Company post of Fort Kiowa. He joined a trading party headed north to the Columbia Fur Company post of Tilton's Fort. When he recovered, Glass left the party and continued west on his own. He arrived at old Fort Henry to find it abandoned, but he kept moving along the Yellowstone River and eventually made it to new Fort Henry.

The men were shocked, and more than a few thought Glass a ghost until they got to touch him. He demanded to see the dogs who had left him to die, but Major Henry, who had heard the commotion, got to him first. Glass described the whole story, and the two went to see Jim.

"Seems you got some explaining to do, Bridger," said the major.

Like the others, Jim could hardly believe his eyes, but he remained silent. He knew he couldn't justify what he'd done. Major Henry came to his defense.

"He's still a pup, Glass."

"Yeah," he finally agreed. "Mebbe he's still a might too wet behind the ears to answer for what he's done. But Fitzgerald ain't," he added hastily. "Where's he?"

"Gone," replied Henry. "Quit and left in early October."

"Damn," muttered Glass, as he walked away.

Jim was left to think about what he'd done. Others blamed Fitzgerald, but in his heart Jim had always known that abandoning Glass was wrong. And worse, here was the major calling him a boy. Those words hurt more than any whupping from Glass ever would have. Jim spent the winter uncertain that he would ever get a chance to prove himself. But circumstances worked in Jim's favor. With trappers at a premium and a battle unfolding between trapping companies for control of the fur trade in the country west of the Missouri, Major Henry wasn't in a position to hold Jim's action against him. Men were needed in the field, and in early 1824, he assigned Bridger to a party charged with opening trade with the Crow along the Bighorn River. It was the last Jim would see of Major Henry, who returned east later that year.

Jim got along with the Crow. He respected their ways and took an interest in their customs. The Crow adopted him into their tribe and called him Casapy, Chief of the Blankets. Jim was with the Crow when Jedidiah Smith and a small party of trappers arrived in February. Smith questioned the Crow about crossing the mountains, where rumor had it, the creeks were choked with beaver. Initially, the Crow refused to give him any information because they didn't want to lose these men whose trade goods they had come to depend on. But Smith's persistence won out, and they described the route he should take. Smith was ready to head out immediately, but few of the Henry-Ashley men wanted to cross the mountain in winter. Jim, who thought highly of Smith, volunteered. In March, the party slipped through what became known as the South Pass, crossed the continental divide and, while they did not know it, entered the Pacific watershed. The rumors proved true. Beaver sign was abundant, and all that was needed for the reaping to begin was for the ice to melt.

The party trapped in the Cache Valley (Bear River Canyon) during the summer. As they gathered around the campfires to prepare pelts, make and repair buckskin outfits and eat, discussions drifted invariably to the course of the Bear River. The others didn't share Jim's opinion, so he was determined to do some exploring on his own.

"You're loco, Jim!" the others exclaimed. "If there ain't more rapids, there's sure to be Injuns."

"What difference where the river heads? Only a fool'd go off on such a danged journey! You're bound to go under, boy."

Jim was no fool, but he was determined to prove that he was a man, and he figured that exploring the Bear River might gain him greater respect among the trappers. So he shrugged off their protests as he built his bull boat, a small vessel made from a willow skeleton and a raw buffalo skin. He slipped it into the river and held tightly to its sides as he rode the rapids out of the Cache Valley. He continued downstream until he came to the river's outlet in a body of water so large that Jim could not see the shore on the far side. He beached the bull boat and walked along the shoreline. He tasted the water and found it salty. He hurried back to camp with the news.

He entered the camp with a broad smile.

"By gum, looks like Blanket Chief found some right friendly Injuns," laughed one. "Don't keep it a secret boy. Where are they?"

"Ain't no Injun princesses at the end of the river," replied Jim. "Just the Pacific Ocean!" he added with a chuckle.

It wasn't really the ocean, but it would be a few years before Jim's discovery was determined to be the Great Salt Lake. Even so, Jim's efforts did cause his superiors to take notice of him.

Later that winter a party of Bannock warriors from a local tribe stole the better part of the trappers' herd of horses. Jim volunteered to pursue the horse thieves and found himself in charge of one of the two groups sent to retrieve the animals. Young Jim Beckwourth had been recently recruited as one of the Henry-Ashley men, and he was placed in Bridger's group. Beckwourth described what happened:

> Tom Fitzpatrick was to charge the Indians and cover Bridger's party, while they stampeded all the horses they could get away with. Everything being in readiness, we rushed in upon the horses, and stampeded from two to three hundred, Fitzpatrick at the same time engaged the Indians, who numbered from three to four hundred. The Indians recovered a great number of the horses from us, but we succeeded in getting off with a number of our own missing, and forty head besides. In the engagement, six of the enemy were killed and scalped, while not one of our party received a scratch.

Fighting Natives was sometimes necessary, but always secondary to the trapping of beavers, and the trappers were always in search of richer territory. In 1826, Jim signed on with Bill Sublette, Jedidiah Smith and David Jackson, who had bought out Ashley, for an expedition to the head of the Yellowstone River. Jim was most interested in going because the region was shrouded in mystery. It was said that a trapper named John Colter had visited there years before. What he had seen convinced him that he had unwittingly stumbled upon an entryway to Hades. The place had since become known as Colter's Hell. Jim didn't put much stock in such stories, thinking that itinerant preachers used the stories to scare their fallen flock into a better life. But he held a different opinion after seeing Colter's Hell, and he shared it with the others when he returned to camp weeks later.

"Boys, as we neared a lake that shattered the sun's rays and scattered them like diamonds, the smell of sulfur was overpowering. When we got closer, we could see the steam rising from the streams. Pits of clay bubbled and spat high into the air. And the streams were so clear that you could see right to the bottom," he added, "if there had been any bottom to see."

"Yup," he declared after a moment of silence. "We been to hell and back!"

They hadn't found beaver along the Yellowstone, and Bill Sublette was worried about his investment, but then news reached him that the Blackfoot were interested in trading. It promised to be risky business because experience had taught the trappers that the Blackfoot were to be feared. Sublette shared the trappers' wariness, but in the competitive fur business, he couldn't afford to pass up an opportunity to deal with them. He called for volunteers to trade with the Blackfoot, sweetening the pot with attractive bonuses. Jim jumped at the opportunity, but soon had cause to reflect on the wisdom of his enthusiasm. While in a Blackfoot camp, he came to blows with some angry braves. Jim held his own, but was taken prisoner. The Blackfoot met in council, and after heated discussion, they decided to kill him. When the warriors went to the lodge where Jim was held, they discovered that he was gone. Rumor had it that a pretty Native woman abetted his flight although Jim never admitted it. Whatever the means of his escape, Jim was fortunate because the Blackfoot warriors shot and dismembered one of the other two volunteers.

Although a trapper faced many hazards, his life wasn't all work and danger. In between the spring and fall hunts there developed what became known as the annual rendezvous. For many a trapper, it was the event that made life in the mountains bearable. It began when the supply trains arrived from the East. With them came the yearly wages, the booze and other foofaraw (trinkets) on which a good portion of those wages were spent freely. For some it was a 10-day drunk, and Jim wasn't out of place among them. Trappers from various companies and some not attached to any employer gathered together for leisurely hunts or to participate in games of skill. Jim wasn't much for the horse races, but he already had something of a reputation with his Hawkins rifle. Rendezvous also attracted friendly Natives, who were anxious to strengthen trading relationships and were usually willing to trade more than just furs.

Jim made the most of these recreational opportunities. Indeed, his free-spirited ways and his fondness for booze and women probably kept him from being promoted to brigade commander (the man in charge of a trapping expedition). But Sublette, Jackson and Smith were all too aware that Jim's knowledge of the Yellowstone country was unsurpassed, so they appointed him brigade guide. In 1830 he led Jedidiah Smith's party through Blackfoot territory south of the Yellowstone River. It was on this expedition that he was nicknamed "Old Gabe." Smith, long known for his biblical ways, thought Jim's usually solemn countenance reminded him of the angel Gabriel. The name was shortened to Gabe, then became Old Gabe—and Jim not yet 30! But he had spent a good many more years in the West than most, and he took to the name, feeling it was a mark of respect, especially since it was given to him by the man he held in such high regard.

Apparently Jim didn't waste all his money on women and booze. Later in 1830 he partnered up with five others, including his good friend Tom Fitzgerald, to buy the old Henry-Ashley outfit from Sublette, Jackson and Smith. They renamed the outfit the Rocky Mountain Fur Company, and Jim was responsible for directing field operations. Unfortunately, it proved an inopportune time to enter the trade as businessmen. A branch of John Jacob Astor's powerful American Fur Company, the Upper Missouri Outfit, under the direction of Kenneth McKenzie, was setting up operation in the region, and McKenzie was determined to drive all his competition out of business.

Upper Missouri Outfit trappers were ordered to follow the Rocky Mountain Fur Company trappers wherever they went. McKenzie flooded the region with below-cost goods, a tactic made possible by Astor's deep pockets, thereby attracting trappers and Natives. It's also possible that McKenzie incited Natives to attack the trappers of the Rocky Mountain Fur Company. Certainly there's a story that Jim Beckwourth, at this time an employee of the Upper Missouri Outfit and living with the Crow, arranged a raid against Tom Fitzgerald. But Beckwourth denied the accusation. The owners of the Rocky Mountain Fur Company were experienced trappers, not conniving businessmen, and they found it difficult to counter McKenzie's underhanded practices.

McKenzie finally stumbled in 1833. The Rocky Mountain Fur Company discovered that the Upper Missouri Outfit was illegally selling booze to the Natives. They brought notice of the practice to the attention of the local Indian agent. He allowed the company to keep its license, but McKenzie's employers shipped him off on a European tour, and later that year, Astor sold out his interest in the company. Victory for Bridger and his partners was short-lived, however. The Rocky Mountain Fur Company broke up in 1834, when increased competition from the northern-based Hudson's Bay Company made it impossible to pay the bills from their eastern suppliers.

Financial problems weren't Jim's only concerns in the early 1830s. In 1831, he learned of Jedidiah Smith's death at the hands of the Comanche. And Jim almost met a similar fate in 1832. He was guiding a brigade and tiring of the dogged efforts of the pursuing Upper Missouri Outfit, so Jim decided to lead his men into Blackfoot country. He thought that his substantial outfit would be safe against all but the largest of Native war parties, while the smaller group that pursued them would be at greater risk. With any luck, the Blackfoot would take care of the Upper Missouri Outfit for them. But Jim's luck was black. He led the men to a Blackfoot village near Pierre's Hole.

"Boys, if any of you are God-fearing men, this'd be a good time to start praying," advised Jim, as warriors suddenly crowded the overlooking cliffs.

"Hold on, Gabe," said Fitzgerald. "Those Injuns are making friendly!"

Jim gave a noncommittal grunt.

Both watched as a small party of Blackfoot approached them. They were carrying a peace pipe. Fitzgerald directed some of the trappers to ride ahead and meet them. Soon several men were seated in a small circle passing around the lighted pipe. Suddenly, a disturbance broke out among the trappers.

"What's troubling Loretto?" asked Jim.

The young Mexican trapper in the brigade was yelling at his wife, a Blackfoot woman who had been captured by the Crow and then purchased by Loretto. Jim watched as she thrust their infant into Loretto's arms and ran to the Blackfoot. She embraced a warrior, who Jim soon learned was her brother.

Jim didn't like the situation one bit. He had been in too many scraps with the Blackfoot to believe that the smoking of a peace pipe was anything more than a ruse to put the trappers off their guard. He rested his rifle across the pommel of his saddle, nudged his horse into a slow trot and made for the Blackfoot. The Native chief advanced to meet him. The pair was within arm's reach of one another when Jim cocked his weapon. The chief leaped forward, grabbed the muzzle and directed it towards the ground, where its load fired harmlessly into the dirt. Jim felt the warrior try to wrest the rifle free but he was determined to hold onto it. Suddenly, two arrows thudded into his back. Jim fell as the rifle slipped from his hands. He landed on his knees and felt the rifle stock connect with the side of his head.

The chief jumped on Jim's horse and rode back to his warriors. They were yelping and shouting and riding in circles. All signs pointed to a big fight, when Loretto dashed unexpectedly to the warriors and gave the child to his wife. The act stunned everyone who was watching, and the Blackfoot chief called a retreat. The warriors slipped back over the cliffs.

Jim suffered through a painful extraction of one of the arrowheads. With no booze, all he could do was chomp down on a thick willow switch and let Fitzgerald yank the arrowhead free. Fitzgerald wasn't successful with the second arrowhead, and it remained embedded in Jim's back for three more years until the missionary Marcus Whitman removed it.

The near-death experience did not deter Jim from trapping in the region. Blackfoot territory was almost the only good beaver country left by the late 1830s. It was either work there or hang up your traps, and Jim wasn't ready to leave the life he loved. He married a Flathead woman named Cora and spent some time with her family. A few outfitters were still looking for experienced guides, and Jim worked for several operations during these years, including the American Fur Company. Jim began to notice that the brigades were smaller and the rendezvous less enthusiastic, and he sensed that the old ways were changing. And it wasn't just because the beaver were nearly all trapped out. In the mid-1830s, missionaries began to arrive, and by the end of the decade, settlers began to trickle west.

Jim made a last effort to finance his own brigade in 1840, traveling all the way to St. Louis to secure backing. But life in the city he once called home wasn't a pleasant experience.

When he finally bumped into an old friend, Jim confessed, "I got myself lost. I been wandering all day long in the canyons of this here city. I seen thousands and thousands of people. And not one of them invited me to sit a while or have a drink or anything!"

Jim's efforts to link up with old partners like Bill Sublette came to nothing, but he managed to strike a two-year deal with Pierre Chouteau, Jr., of the prominent St. Louis fur-trading family, and quickly scampered back to the woods.

By 1840 and 1841 a steady stream of settlers was making its way west on what became known as the Oregon/California Trail. Jim saw good business in trading with them, and the realization made him think about hanging up his traps. But it was when he bumped into his old friend Tom Fitzgerald in 1842 that he made his mind up. Tom had given up trapping to work as a guide.

"The future is with the settlers, Ol' Gabe," he declared.

Jim couldn't disagree, and in 1843, he said farewell to trapping and teamed up with old friend and fellow trapper/trader Louis Vasquez to open Fort Bridger on the Black Fork of the Green River. It was an unassuming post on two acres of stockaded land, but at 400 miles west of Fort Laramie, it was ideally located for settlers whose depleted supplies and damaged equipment needed addressing before their final push into California or Oregon. Jim spent most of the summer giving advice on routes and territory.

Jim also had time for the Rocky Mountain hunters and trappers who gathered at the post. There weren't many more than a few dozen mountain men left. And Jim lamented their quality when a trapping party he led refused to fight a band of Sioux braves. The men had good reason to steer clear of the

Fort Bridger, from an 1858 edition of *Harper's Weekly*; opened in 1843 on the Black Fork of the Green River

Sioux, who outnumbered them, but odds weren't a consideration for Jim. His blood ran hot as he recalled the good old days when fighting Natives was part of trapping life.

Throughout the mid-1840s, Jim continued to roam the territory west of the Wasatch Range. He made several journeys into the Great Basin adding to his vast knowledge of the region. Rarely did he travel with more than a few friends and his wife. But in 1846, his wife Cora was bitten by a wolf and died of rabies. In 1848, he trekked into Ute country to the south and returned with one of their women. He married her, but she died during childbirth within a year.

Jim married once more and almost died because of it. He was leading a buffalo hunt in Shoshone Snake River country in 1848. The hunters encountered the powerful Chief Washakie's band. Jim had long known Washakie and even had a Shoshone name, Peejatowahooten, the Mysterious Medicine Chief who could change buffalo pelts into kettles, knives and sometimes rifles. Washakie invited the hunters to stay in the winter camp. Washakie had a beautiful daughter named Little Fawn. She was much desired by many braves, and Washakie had arranged for her to marry the war chief Ear of the Fox. Little Fawn had other ideas. One night she hung a pair of moccasins outside Jim's lodge, a signal that she wished to marry him. Jim realized that Little Fawn's actions placed Washakie in an awkward position, so he ignored the moccasins. Washakie also ignored what his daughter had done, hoping that he might resolve the problem after Jim left. But Ear of the Fox felt insulted, and he wanted to remove the stain from his honor. So one evening, he attacked Jim. The encounter was long remembered by the Shoshone, perhaps because of its violence, as is related in their telling of the story:

> They fought a terrible fight. They started out fighting on horseback, and their horses stumbled through the village tight together. Then they fell to the ground and rolled over and over, hitting and kicking, biting and gouging, battling like animals or demons. Finally they were on their feet and slashing at each other with knives. Their buckskins were ripped to pieces, and both of them were covered with blood. But at last the fight ended, and the Mysterious Medicine Chief's blade was buried deep in the chest of Ear of the Fox.

At 44, Jim still had plenty of spunk. He returned after the death of his second wife to collect Little Fawn, who he renamed Mary. Together they returned to a busy Fort Bridger.

Portrait of Shoshone chief Washakie (1804–1900). Washakie rescued one of Jim's brigades when it was pinned down by hostile Blackfoot. Washakie was a prominent warrior and did not hesitate to raise his war club against the traditional Native enemies of his people. However, Washakie was an advocate of peace with the white man, and when he became chief in 1840, he tried to forge good relations with the newcomers. He urged his people to help the settlers who crossed Shoshone land in present-day Utah and Wyoming. He wasn't always successful in restraining Shoshone warriors, but western pioneers recognized his efforts. Before he died, some 9000 settlers signed a document that attested to the assistance provided by Washakie and his people during their travels west.

With the news of gold in California, settlers were passing by in increasing numbers. So was the military. In August 1849, Captain Howard Stansbury of the United States Corps of Topographical Engineers arrived with the responsibility of improving the wagon routes west.

"We're looking to survey a trail to the Humboldt River," Stansbury explained to Jim. "Greenwood's Cut-Off and the California Trail through Fort Hall are too far north. And we want to avoid the Great Salt Desert to the south. Any ideas?"

Stansbury asked the question without enthusiasm. Jim, approaching 50 but looking more like 60, hardly appeared to be the fount of knowledge Stansbury had been led to believe he was.

Jim unrolled a buffalo hide, grabbed a piece of charcoal and scratched out a route that slipped between Bear Lake and the northern reach of the Wasatch Range.

"There's your new road," declared Jim.

Stansbury looked at the map, then to Jim. He wasn't certain about what he saw.

"Why don't you join the party as a guide?"

Jim agreed, and a few weeks later, Stansbury admitted, "We found it to be as the guide had stated."

Stansbury hired Bridger again in 1850, when the engineers were looking to develop a western all-weather route. Jim helped them lay out a route that stretched from the South Platte River to Fort Bridger, including Bridger's Pass south of the Antelope Hills. Stansbury's glowing report to his superiors did much to spread Jim Bridger's reputation in the East.

Throughout the 1850s, Jim found himself entangled in problems with the Mormons. The Mormons wanted access to trade west of Fort Laramie, but Fort Bridger had it mostly tied up. Jim knew something of the Mormons' determined ways. So in the fall of 1852, to protect his interests, he took out title to Fort Bridger, which fell within the newly formed Utah Territory

(1851). Title proved insufficient. In the summer of 1853, officials in Salt Lake City ordered him out of the territory. When
Jim refused, Governor Brigham Young, also leader of the Mormons, ordered Bridger's arrest. In August, a contingent of 150
Utah Territorial Militia (Nauvoo Legion) showed up at Fort
Bridger. Jim was nearby visiting some settlers, and Mary greeted
the soldiers, assuring them that any attack would be followed
by a war with the Shoshone. The threat was enough to discour-
age the commanding officer, who soon led his men northeast
to deal with the Green River ferrymen, another group that had
roused Mormon anger.

Jim hurried to Fort Laramie and demanded that action be
taken against the Mormons. The commanding officer assured
him that the matter would be addressed when the federally
appointed non-Mormon governor arrived. Jim left and spent
the winter with his Shoshone relatives. Washakie offered to
lead his 1200 braves against the Mormons, but Jim thought it
was best to let the government deal with the situation. It was
not in Jim's nature to be bullied, so he set up Bridger's Ferry
west of Fort Laramie on the North Platte River and east of
a competing Mormon operation at Upper Crossing. Jim was
sour over losing the Green River trade, but Bridger's Ferry
brought him a measure of satisfaction, especially when it
forced the closure of the Mormon Ferry within a year. He hired
river men thrown out of business by Mormon operations on
the Green River and left them to run the ferry while he headed
to Missouri, where he purchased a 640-acre farm near Westport. The old Thatcher farm was home for the rest of his life,
although perhaps not by choice. His partner, Louis Vasquez
had sold his old home of Fort Bridger, a sale that Jim con-
tended was done without his knowledge or consent.

Jim was often away from home. Throughout 1855–56, he
served as a Powder River country guide for Sir George Gore,
a wealthy Irish nobleman. Gore hired Bridger as much for his

Fort Laramie, at the junction of the Laramie and North Platte Rivers; purchased by the army in 1849 to figure in America's westward expansion

stories as his expertise. He enjoyed Jim's stories late in the evening after dinner and over wine. Surely some of Jim's tales were accurate descriptions of his trapping and Native fighting days. But Old Gabe couldn't keep out the occasional tall tale, such as the one about the race of giants who lived on an island in the middle of Great Salt Lake and used elephants as ponies.

Jim also enjoyed listening to Gore read Shakespeare's plays and the narratives of great historians.

It was easy money working for Gore, but eventually, the nobleman returned to Ireland. Jim made for Washington, where James Buchanan, the new president, invited him to share his view of the Mormon situation. Buchanan was more inclined to act on the Mormon matter than was his predecessor, and he fulfilled previous promises to send a non-Mormon governor to the territory. He also decided to establish a military detachment in Utah Territory. By the time they marched west in July 1857, Jim had returned to Fort Laramie. There, Assistant Quartermaster P.W.I. Plympton asked Jim if he would serve as the governor's guide into Utah. Jim agreed and returned to Bridger's Ferry to await the troops. They arrived in July 1857.

Jim guided eight companies of the Tenth Infantry under the command of Colonel E.B. Alexander to the Green River in late September, only days after Utah Territory declared war on the United States. They arrived to discover that the Nauvoo Legion had burned much of the territory east of Salt Lake Valley, including Fort Bridger. Jim advised Alexander to push on to Salt Lake City, but without orders and in the face of well-founded rumors that the Nauvoo Legion numbered as many as 6000 strong, Alexander refused. Jim hurried back East in search of a ranking officer who could authorize an advance. He found Colonel Albert S. Johnston along the Sweetwater River. He had recently arrived from action in Texas. Jim guided Johnston to Black's Fork before winter set in. Johnston was so impressed by the grizzled man in buckskins that he appointed Jim chief guide for the expedition and gave him the rank of major.

The army was forced to remain at Black's Fork throughout the winter, but in the spring, Jim led the soldiers deep into Utah Territory. Their arrival was anticlimactic. Brigham Young, upon hearing that the Shoshone might join the soldiers, had ordered a retreat of the Nauvoo Legion. When Jim entered Salt Lake City with the troops in late June, it was deserted.

The matter came to a close when the Mormons accepted the new governor, Alfred Cumming.

Jim returned to his Westport farm, where he remained for the winter with his children. Mary had recently died in childbirth. In the spring of 1859, Jim was again working for the United States Corps of Topographical Engineers. He remained so employed for two years, guiding them through the Yellowstone country. Rumors suggest that Jim found gold in the Black Hills during this expedition, but that military officials ordered him to keep it secret. No one wanted trouble with the Sioux, who controlled the region.

Jim's skills proved invaluable on the expedition, although haughty officers often couldn't see beyond his gruff appearance. Such was the case when the expedition reached a swollen Snake River.

"Only way to ford the river is to build a bull boat," declared Jim.

"You've been hired as a guide, not an engineer, Bridger," spat Raynolds, the captain in charge. He ordered a raft built. When it was launched, it overturned in the fast current, and one soldier drowned.

"Jim," said Raynolds, finally, "you go ahead and build that bull boat."

"Only if you stay in your tent and outta my hair!" barked Jim.

Raynolds agreed. Jim built the bull boat, slipped into the vessel and quickly forded the river with a cable in tow. Once the cable was fastened to the other side, ferrying the men across was an easy matter. He left Raynolds until last, when the buffalo hide covering of the bull boat was wet and stinky. Upon safely reaching the far shore, Raynolds called his men together and said a prayer thanking God.

"Damn his holy hide!" muttered Jim. "He never once mentioned Jim Bridger!"

Jim Bridger in his 60s, when he worked as a scout for troops ordered to bring the Plains Natives under control

Jim continued to work for the army throughout the 1860s, taking time to guide the occasional emigrant train or to rest with his family in Westport. In early 1865, he was appointed chief scout for General Patrick Connor's Powder River Expedition against the hostile Cheyenne and Sioux, who were harassing prospectors en route to the Montana gold fields. By this time Jim had acquired such a reputation for storytelling that even frontier newspapers were warning readers about Old Gabe's tall tales. But Jim always found a willing audience. On one occasion on the shores of Lake De Smet, he stopped to have a mug-up with a group of young officers.

"Remember that creek with the coal beds washed clean?" asked Jim. "Well the whole bottom of this lake is like that— pure, solid coal. One of these days I'm coming back here and make myself a heap of money."

"How are you going to mine it underwater?" asked one of the officers.

"Mine it!" coughed Jim, as he sputtered out a mouthful of coffee. "Ain't gonna be no mining. There's no pile in that. But there's a flowing oil seep off that bluff, and this here water's so full of alkali you can toss in an egg and it won't sink."

"No one's going to come to see an egg float," laughed an officer.

"Boys, it ain't about floating eggs," protested Jim. "If you dug a ditch to run that oil in, then tunnelled under through to coal, then set your tunnel afire and got the whole lake boiling, what would you get when boiling up oil and alkali water?" asked Jim.

"Soap?" guessed one.

"Damn straight, soap," barked Jim. "You could make enough soap here in one summer to last the whole country more than a hundred years."

The lake was two miles long and three-quarters of a mile wide, and it would have made quite a cauldron. Over the dying embers of their fire, the officers discussed future fortunes to be made in keeping America clean!

The problem with a storyteller who was liberal with the truth was that listeners never knew what to believe. Patrick Connor, who was already suspicious of Jim because of his Native wives, harbored a fear that he might guide them right into an ambush. Connor found nothing reassuring when he heard that Jim was feeding his men stories about a medicine wolf. Old Gabe never exactly explained what a medicine wolf was, but when he heard it howling just outside the camp, he told the officers that it was sure to bring trouble. While Connor fretted that this was more evidence of Jim's Native ways, the men mostly laughed at his superstitions. Soon after Jim heard the howling medicine wolf, the expedition suffered a series of setbacks, including harsh weather and Native attacks. It ended in failure.

After that disastrous Powder River Expedition, the American government decided to make treaty with the hostile Natives. The treaty commissioners were optimistic about success, but Jim knew the Natives and was less certain.

"Injuns always want to talk peace when winter's holding them down, when there's only cottonwood bark for the ponies," Jim suggested to one young officer. "Wait till spring and the ponies get fat on new grass. Hear what they says then. Long as the Bozeman Trail runs through Sioux country, there'll be trouble."

Jim was proven right at the Fort Laramie treaty negotiations held in the spring of 1866. When the Sioux learned that Colonel Henry Carrington was marching troops to establish posts along the Bozeman Trail that linked Julesburg, Colorado, and Virginia City, Montana, and cut through Sioux hunting territory in the Powder River country, the Sioux exploded out of the council. Led by Red Cloud, they went to war. Ironically, Jim was Carrington's guide into the region. The American government, anticipating peace and wanting to cut costs, had issued orders to Carrington to fire Bridger. But Carrington had come to depend on Old Gabe's expertise, and he wrote back a terse message: "Impossible of execution."

Jim worked for Carrington throughout 1867. He rode north with Jim Beckwourth to solidify relations with the Crow. He was at Fort Phil Kearney that fateful day, when Red Cloud's warriors annihilated the arrogant young Captain William

Fetterman's detachment. When braves pinned down a wood train outside the fort, Jim counseled Carrington that his response should be a cautious one. Carrington agreed, but Fetterman felt that the Sioux needed to be taught a lesson. He led his 80 men into an ambush, where all were killed. Eventually, Red Cloud forced the United States to accept his terms. Jim was discharged soon after the treaty negotiations, and it was the last time he worked for the army.

In 1871, Jim returned to Westport. He operated a store for a time, but retirement was forced on him as his health failed, and he lost his eyesight. He remained popular with the locals, especially the children, who called him Grandpa Bridger. Jim died at a friend's house on July 17, 1881.

CHAPTER FOUR

James Beckwourth
1800–1866

JAMES BECKWOURTH* was born a slave, likely in 1800. His father, Sir Jennings Beckwith, was the son of an aristocrat who could trace his ancestry back to the time of the Battle of Hastings nearly 600 years before. His mother, her name forgotten by history, was a mulatto slave. Jim was born in Frederick County, Virginia, but he never got to know the place. Financial setbacks diminished his father's small fortune, and Jim was still a toddler when the Beckwith family moved west to Missouri. While most of Beckwith's slaves were sold before the move, Jim remained with the family because his father considered him more of a son than chattel. Beckwith eventually purchased 1280 acres bounded by the Missouri and Mississippi rivers and called it The Point.

The carefree existence Jim enjoyed at The Point nurtured his lifelong ease in the backwoods. The nearest settlement of

---

*James Beckwourth's birth surname was Beckwith. In his autobiography it was changed to Beckwourth, which has since remained the popular spelling of the mountain man's surname.

St. Charles was miles away, and Jim spent his days in fragrant forests rather than on dusty streets. And he didn't want for companionship. He had 13 siblings and neighbors that homesteaded nearby. But Jim discovered that not all the local folk were friendly. The Natives in the area were none too pleased about white settlers living in their traditional territories. Beckwith and his neighbors joined together and built a blockhouse, a fortified dwelling of squared logs, for protection. Most days everyone gathered there to protect themselves from a Native attack.

Young Jim was ignorant of the dangers posed by angry Natives, and such gatherings were mostly fun and games for him. But a dose of frontier reality awaited him one day when his father sent him to a nearby mill with a sack of corn for grinding. Jim, about 10 or 11, was pleased that his father thought him responsible enough for the task, and he was eager to share his pleasure with some friends who lived along the road to the mill. As he rode, he imagined the envious smiles of the children still too young to be allowed to undertake such a job. He smiled when he thought about spending a few minutes talking with the older boys who also shouldered such responsibilities. As Jim approached the fence that separated the house from the road, his smile gave way to a frown. The place was silent, and that was mighty strange.

"Hallo!" he called.

No one replied, and then Jim saw why. Lying on the ground in front of the house were the family's eight children. Jim's breath came in fitful gasps when he saw that their throats were cut and their scalps were gone. None had been spared, not even the infant. He pulled his eyes away and looked to the doorway, where he saw the mother and father. Dark pools of blood had formed on the wooden stoop below them. Jim sagged over the neck of his horse and threw up his breakfast.

Jim rushed home and told his father. Soon 11 men were in pursuit of the Natives. They returned a couple of days later with 18 Native scalps.

"The backwoods men fought the savage in Indian style, and it was scalp for scalp between them," as Jim put it.

Jim received limited formal education in his youth. In his teens, he was indentured to a blacksmith, but he found the apprenticeship constraining. Following an especially nasty fight with his master, Jim fled. Local constables tracked him down and detained him to await word from his father. Although Beckwith wanted Jim to continue with his apprenticeship, Jim stubbornly declared the relationship over. When his father proposed to set him up in a local business, Jim revealed his desire to go west. The elder Beckwith considered his 19-year-old son and consented.

"He admonished me with some wholesome precepts, gave me $500 in cash together with a good horse, saddle and bridle and bade me God speed upon my journey," said Jim.

At 22, Jim signed on with Colonel James Johnson's 1822 expedition up the Fever River in Illinois. Johnson sought to make treaty with the local Sac so that he could exploit minerals on their territory. Negotiations were successful, and Jim enjoyed a profitable 18 months among the Sac. When he left the expedition, he traveled to New Orleans and worked on the docks, where he picked up yellow fever. He sweated out the worst of it before going home to his father's house to recover.

Jim faced more challenges of frontier life on his next adventure. When Jim heard that General William Ashley and his partner Major Andrew Henry were seeking men for an overland expedition to the Rocky Mountains, Jim was interested. But he had heard that Moses Harris, the mountain man acting as the Henry-Ashley agent, had a reputation for cold-heartedness. Jim wouldn't place his life in Harris' hands until he met with the man and took his measure.

"Harris, I'm thinking of accompanying you on this trip," said Jim.

"Very well, Jim," replied Harris, as he looked the young man over. "Do you think you can stand it?"

"I don't know, but I'm going to try. But I wish you to bear one thing in mind: if I should give out on the road, and you offer to leave me to perish, as you have the name of doing, and if I have strength to raise and cock my rifle, I shall certainly bring you to a halt," Jim stated brashly.

Harris looked Jim in the eye as he replied, "Jim, you may precede me the entire way and take your own jog. If I direct the path and give you the lead, it will be your own fault if you tire out."

"That satisfies me," answered Jim.

Knowing where he stood with Harris, Jim joined Ashley's western-bound party at Fort Atkinson, Nebraska, in November 1824. For the first time in his life, he traveled as a free man; his father had freed him in July with a Deed of Emancipation. With winter approaching, it was a poor time of year to head west, and Ashley had difficulty attracting enough men. But he had to get supplies to the Ashley-Henry men already at Henry's Fork on the Green River. Those who did sign on were soon reconsidering their decision. The party suffered terribly along the route. Snow fell within weeks, and by December, most of their supplies were gone, which was just as well because few horses were left alive to pack the goods. It was anticipated that game would supplement the rations, but the party rarely saw any. The fortuitous arrival of a group of kind-hearted Pawnee Natives from the Loup River saved the group from certain starvation. On those rare occasions when they brought down game, Jim bragged that he was usually the successful hunter. However, he didn't always know what he was shooting at.

"I climbed a tree to get a fairer elevation of the ground," described Jim on one expedition. "Looking around from my elevated position, I perceived some large, dark-colored animal grazing on the side of a hill, some mile and a half distant. I was determined to have a shot at him, whatever he might be. I therefore approached, with the greatest precaution, to within fair rifle-shot distance, scrutinizing him very closely and still unable to make out what he was. I could see no horns; and if he was a bear, I thought him an enormous one. I took sight at him over my faithful rifle, which had never failed me, and then set it down to contemplate the huge animal still further. Finally, I resolved to let fly; taking good aim, I pulled the trigger, the rifle cracked and then I made rapid retreat towards the camp. After running about 200 yards and hearing nothing in movement behind me, I ventured to look round, and to my great joy, I saw the animal had fallen."

Jim returned to camp, where he found Ashley.

"Have you shot anything, Jim?"

"Yes sir," he replied.

"What have you shot?"

"Two deer and something else."

"And what is the something else?"

"I do not know, sir," admitted Jim.

"What did he look like?" asked Ashley. "Had he horns?"

"I saw no horns, sir."

"What color was the animal?"

"You can see him, general," sighed Jim, "by climbing yonder tree."

Ashley ascended the tree, took out his spyglass and looked to the far hill.

"Jim! A buffalo, by heavens!"

It was the first of many buffalo that Jim would shoot. As the party continued west along the South Platte River, Jim's relationship with Ashley took a sour turn, and the pair butted heads. Perhaps Ashley couldn't be faulted for the cold or the lack of game, but the man had a temper that found voice in some of the foulest language that Jim had ever heard. He often took Jim to task in an unreasonable manner suggesting to the young black man that his employer saw him as something less than a paid personal servant. Jim eventually gave vent to his frustration, and a poor, stubborn packhorse, which Ashley had ordered him to rein in, received the worst of the abuse. His hands frozen from fiddling with the icy pack ropes, Jim finally grabbed his hammer and drove its head into the animal's skull.

"There, take that!" exclaimed Jim. "I only wish you were General Ashley."

"You do, do you?"

Jim recognized the voice that came from the nearby bushes. A volley of curses followed the question, but Jim didn't flinch.

"What I said I meant," shouted Jim, defiantly, "and it makes no odds whether you heard it or not."

"You are an infernal scoundrel, and I'll shoot you," said Ashley, as he cocked his rifle and leveled it at Jim.

Jim cocked his rifle, and the two faced each other, eyes locked.

"General," said Jim, "you have addressed language to me which I allow no man to use, and unless you retract that last epithet, you or I must surely die."

"I will acknowledge that it was language that never should be used to a man, but when I am angry, I am apt to speak hastily. But I will make you suffer for this," he added.

"Not in your service, general," replied Jim. "You can take your horse now, and do what you please with him. I will return to St. Louis."

Jim was prepared to strike out on his own and possibly head back East to see his family. Only his desire to see the Rocky Mountains prevented him from doing so and he agreed to stay on. He was after all out on the frontier, and despite his cockiness, Jim knew a man alone could not contend as well with the vagaries of nature and hostile Natives.

As the party approached the Green River, Ashley divided the men into four groups, each directed to trap different streams. Jim found himself in the group headed by James Clyman, a man with a reputation for fighting Natives. Clyman's experience would be needed. While the group camped on a tributary of the Green River, some apparently friendly Blackfoot warriors approached to trade. The trappers knew of the Blackfoot's violent reputation, and most of them were on pins and needles. Jim was suspicious of the warriors' interest in the party's rifles, and when he went to bed, he made sure his own weapon was close at hand. In the middle of the night, a gunshot woke the camp. Jim heard one of his companions, Le Brache, scream. He reached for his rifle, and his hand fell on the hand of a Native who was trying to steal it. Jim jerked the rifle away and crawled towards La Brache, who had a tomahawk embedded in his skull. Thinking quickly, Jim scattered the embers of the fire to douse completely what little light it gave. The Blackfoot slipped away into the darkness. Clyman urged the men to pack up as best they could, and he led them to the open prairie. The short journey was a harrowing one, with musket balls and arrows flying all around the fleeing men. No one returned for the $4000 worth of beaver pelts, 40 horses and other merchandise left behind, which was a considerable loss.

Jim was in the Rocky Mountains by the summer of 1825. He trapped with Clyman, Jedidiah Smith and James Bridger, who each possessed an intimate knowledge of the trade and the region and a willingness to share it. Jim's pelts went back to his employers, but he could never trap enough beaver to pay off the outfit supplied to him and the goods he had received since he signed on with Henry-Ashley. So, Jim bolted to a competing trading outfit, the Upper Missouri Outfit, owned by John Jacob Astor's American Fur Company. He was soon directed by the local employer of the outfit, the "King of the Missouri," Kenneth McKenzie, to make an alliance with the Crow. McKenzie expected that having an agent among the Crow would increase the Natives' willingness to trade with his company.

With the assistance of a grizzled old trader who knew how to spin a yarn, Jim convinced Crow chief Big Bowl that he was the chief's long lost son who had been captured by the Cheyenne and sold to whites years before. Some doubted Jim's story, but however it came about, he became a member of a Crow band by 1828. It was a good relationship for both parties. As McKenzie hoped, the Upper Missouri Outfit assured itself unchallenged access to the tribe's furs, and the Crow had their choice of desirable trade goods. While Jim enjoyed a certain status because of his position, he wasn't content to remain a trader among the Crow. It wasn't long before he joined his first raiding party against the Blood and won honors for himself.

> *Our chief ordered a charge upon them. I advanced directly upon their line and had struck down my man before the others came up. The others, after making a furious advance that threatened annihilation to our new foes, curveted aside in Indian fashion, thus losing the effect of a first onset. I corrected this unwarlike custom. On this occasion, seeing me engaged hand to hand with the enemy's whole force, they immediately came to my assistance, and the opposing party was quickly dispatched. I despoiled my victim of his gun, lance, war-club, bow and quiver of arrows. Now I was the greatest man in the party, for I had killed the first warrior.*

Jim was singled out for honors in the celebrations that followed and claimed that the fame allowed him to lead future raids. A particular battle in the fall of 1833 against the Blackfoot stands out. On this occasion, the outnumbered Blackfoot proved stubborn, and the Crow chief Long Hair declared that his warriors should pull back. He was confident of victory but feared it would claim too many Crow lives.

"No! Hold!" barked Jim. "Warriors, listen! If these old men cannot fight, let them retire with the women and children. We can kill every one of these Black Feet: then let us do it. If we attempt to run from here, we shall be shot in the back and lose more warriors than to fight and kill them all. If we are killed, our friends who love us here will mourn our loss, while those in the spirit land will sing and rejoice to welcome us there, if we ascend to them dying like braves. The Great Spirit has sent these enemies here for us to slay; if we do not slay them, he will be angry with us and will never suffer us to conquer our enemies again. He will drive off all our buffaloes and will whiten the grass on the prairies. No, warriors! We will fight as long as one of them survives. Come and follow me, and I will show you how the braves of the great white chief fight their enemies!"

The Crow respected Jim's words of bravado, and the hundreds of warriors who had gathered around him shouted in unison one of the handful of Crow names he was to earn over the years.

"Enemy of Horses! Enemy of Horses! Lead us, and we will follow you to the spirit land!"

Forty Crow died in the attack, but Jim was not one of them. The Crow took 160 scalps and many supplies, and Jim was again celebrated for his leadership.

Beckwourth's reputation as a warrior, or a war chief as he called himself, and his link with the Upper Missouri Outfit made him much sought after as a husband. He married at least seven Crow women and had his eyes set on an eighth before coming to the shocking realization that his charms were not irresistible. Jim set his sights on Pine Leaf, an attractive young woman who had come to his attention because of her participation in raids. Jim thought she had few equals among the warriors. He knew that she had pledged to remain chaste until she had killed 100 enemies to avenge the death of her brother, who had died during an attack. But Jim thought that the determined woman must have been close to her goal. When he spoke to her about his intentions, Pine Leaf advised him that she would become his wife when the pine leaves turned yellow. Happily, Jim thought of autumn. It was days later before he realized that pine leaves never turn color.

Jim left the Crow sometime in 1834, probably after a falling out with the Upper Missouri Outfit. In late 1833, he had been accused of participating in a raid on a trading party led by Thomas Fitzpatrick of the Rocky Mountain Fur Company. Fitzpatrick complained to McKenzie, but it's quite possible that the "King of the Missouri," who was eager to undermine his competition, was in on the attack. However, even McKenzie worried that Jim liked fighting a little too much. The problem was that too much violence undermined company profits. The Crow preferred fighting to trapping, and the more the Crow raided, the less other tribes trapped. The Upper Missouri Outfit did not renew Jim's contract.

In the summer of 1836, Jim headed for St. Louis. Frontier towns were used to strange sights, but Jim stood out. He rode bareback, continued to dress in the Crow style of leather clothes and moccasins and his long hair was braided into two thick plaits.

Jim had no difficulty finding a saloon, and he was bending his elbow at its bar when he heard a voice growl, "There's the Crow."

He spun around to see Tom Fitzgerald and four companions approaching him. Jim recognized one by his reputation for being violent and mean and with no match in St. Louis. Jim's eyes didn't rest long on the men's faces; they were drawn instead to the knives the men brandished.

"Heard you were in town, Crow," snarled Fitzgerald. "I was glad to hear it 'cause as I recall, we got some business to settle."

Jim knew that Fitzgerald held him responsible for the Crow raid on his Rocky Mountain Fur Trading outfit. Jim claimed that the charge was false, but he also knew that this wasn't the time for objections.

"Far as I'm concerned, there ain't no business to settle," replied Jim. "But I won't let words get in the way of a good fight," he added as he leapt from his stool and pulled out his own knife.

Jim was about ready to give the Crow war cry and charge when a constable, who happened to be in the saloon, grabbed Jim's shoulder.

"There's not going to be any trouble in here, boys," said the constable. "And any man who doesn't sheathe his knife is going to cool his heels in the calaboose."

Fitzgerald's friends obviously knew something about the local jail, and so were the first to leave.

"The Rockies ain't big enough to hide you, Crow," warned Fitzgerald as he followed them. "I'll clear the books yet."

"How about right now?" declared Jim as he made for the door.

"Another step and it'll be a long time before you see the Rockies again, mister," shouted the constable.

Jim looked at the door and then to the constable and decided to return to the bar.

Jim didn't remain in St. Louis much longer. While he was concerned for his safety, he simply didn't like the bustle of the growing city. By 1837 Jim was back in the Rocky Mountains, hoping that the Upper Missouri Outfit would reconsider its decision about his employability. Jim visited his Crow friends and family, and while he was there, band members fell ill from smallpox. Some suspected that Jim had brought the disease with him on some infected blankets. Jim denied it, but he didn't leave the Crow on the best of terms. When he learned that the Upper Missouri Outfit remained uninterested in his services, he settled his debts and headed for Florida.

The Seminole in Florida had been causing the American government problems since the United States had acquired the territory in 1819. Despite treaties, the Seminole refused to relocate in order to allow their land to be opened for settlement. The Seminole Wars erupted in 1835. It was a bloody affair; 2000 white soldiers and settlers died, and 4000 Seminoles were forcibly moved west by war's end in 1842. Beckwourth heard that General Edmund Gaines was recruiting men for the fight. In need of work and thinking that he might gain some notoriety, he signed up as a civilian employee. He was stationed at Fort Brooke, Florida.

With his usual flair for exaggeration, Jim boasted that he was a captain during the war, and in later years, some used this title when referring to him. As a contracted civilian he had no rank, and he did little fighting. He was a muleteer (broke mules), a teamster and an express rider. Evidently, he was good at his work because he was paid more than others who did similar jobs. Jim witnessed the Battle of Okeechobee on December 25, 1837, the fiercest fight of the war. The Seminoles were outnumbered more than two to one, but their casualties were fewer than the army's. Jim was charged with carrying the victory dispatches to Tampa Bay.

Each time he passed a fort, he shouted, "Victory! Victory!" Officers and men poured out of the forts, impatient to hear the news.

But he confessed, "I could not see that O-ke-cho-be was much of a victory: Indeed, I shrewdly suspected that the enemy had the advantage; but it was called a victory by the soldiers, and they were the best qualified to decide."

After the battle, there was a lull in the fighting, and Jim found the inactivity tiring. He couldn't even steal horses, a pastime he had enjoyed while living with the Crow, because the Seminole, he lamented, had no horses worth the effort. And while he enjoyed the warm weather, he came to dislike traveling through the swampy territory with its dense and tangled undergrowth. He was forever on the lookout for alligators, snakes and hostile Natives. Jim quit his position with the army and was back in St. Louis by the summer of 1838.

Jim wasn't long in St. Louis when fur traders Louis Vasquez and Andrew Sublette came calling with a proposition. They operated a trading post called Fort Vasquez on the South Platte River, and they wanted Jim to be its agent-in-charge. Vasquez and Sublette were looking for an edge in the competitive world of fur trading. The American Fur Company and the Bent brothers, along with their partner Ceran St. Vrain, controlled most of the trading in the region, and it was not easy to convince Natives to change trading partners. Vasquez and Sublette were hopeful that Beckwourth's experience with the Crow and his knowledge of Native ways could bring success to their trading operation.

Jim was pleased with the offer from his old friend Vasquez, and because he was aware that paying opportunities in fur trade territory were increasingly limited, he accepted. In July, he joined his new employers and headed up the Missouri River by steamboat. From Independence, Missouri, they continued west on the Santa Fe Trail. Jim became ill from sunstroke on the journey and rode in a wagon until he recovered. Eventually, the Rocky Mountains appeared on the horizon, and the party headed north until they reached Fort Vasquez.

The trading partners realized quickly that they had chosen well. Jim knew that a little humility and a lot of bravado helped when trading with the Natives. He was working in their world and knew that the Natives "consider the country they inhabit as the gift of the Great Spirit, and they resent in their hearts the invasion of the immigrant just as much as any

Ceran St. Vrain, who with Charles Bent formed one of the most important fur-trading companies in operation before the mid-19th century.

civilized people would, if another nation, without permission, should cross their territory," he explained.

But Natives also respected courage, and Jim ventured without fear into the Crow and Cheyenne camps to trade. He even joined in the warriors' dances and recited his coups. Jim also had a good feel for the use of firewater in dealing with the Natives. Negotiations were usually opened with a small kettle of booze. If the trader settled on the right amount, he might cut himself a good deal. Too little or too much firewater and he might find his neck cut by an angry or drunk Native. Under Jim's leadership, the partnership enjoyed a few good years. But the winter of 1839–40 proved difficult, and the firm sold out in 1840.

Beckwourth didn't even have the time for one of his solitary rambles before Bent, St. Vrain and Company offered him work. While the western trading operations covered large amounts of territory, the fraternity was a small one, and Jim's success with the Upper Missouri Outfit and Sublette and Vasquez had not gone unnoticed by potential employers. A man who could improve a company's bottom line was in demand, and Jim named his own salary. By late summer he was trading at Bent's Fort at Laramie Fork. When the Natives learned he was there, they showed up in increasing numbers to trade. Occasionally, even Jim's skill wasn't enough to prevent matters getting out of hand, as happened with Old Smoke's band, as he describes:

> I gave them a grand entertainment, which seemed to tickle their tastes highly. They kept up their carousal until they had parted with 2000 robes and had no more remaining. They then demanded whiskey, and I refused it. 'No trust,' the motto we see inscribed on every low drinking saloon in St. Louis, is equally our system in dealing with the Indians. They became infuriated at my refusal and clamored and threatened if I persisted. I knew it was no use to give way, so I adhered to my resolution. Thereupon, they commenced firing upon the store and showered the bullets through every assailable point. The windows were shot entirely out, and the assailants swore vengeance against the Crow.

Jim, "the Crow," spent a sleepless night with his loaded rifles by his side, but the Natives never stormed the post. Bent and St. Vrain arrived the next day and applauded his fortitude

Lithograph of Bent's Fort, taken from T.F. Rodenbough's "From Everglade to Canon with the Second Dragoons, 1836–75." Bent, St. Vrain and Company built the important trading post on the Arkansas River west of the Purgatoire (in present-day Colorado) in 1833. Also known as Fort William because William Bent supervised the construction of the adobe fortress and later managed it, Bent's Fort served both western-bound settlers traveling the Santa Fe Trail and Native peoples of the southern Great Plains. After the death of Charles Bent in 1847 and the retirement of Ceran St. Vrain in 1849, William became sole owner of the fort. That same year he tried to sell Bent's Fort to the American government, but when they would not pay the price he wanted, William destroyed it.

as their wide eyes scanned the great pile of furs that Jim had acquired. They were so impressed that when they expanded into Arapaho territory, they selected Jim to undertake the enterprise. Jim agreed, and the result was a great success. But even as he returned to Bent's Fort with the season's furs, Jim was contemplating moving on. He was never comfortable working for others, and he was aware that his efforts and his risks were bringing in great profits for his employers. Jim counted his savings and considered going into business for himself.

In 1841 he headed for Taos, New Mexico, a five-day ride to the south. Taos was the unofficial southern headquarters of the mountain men. Jim entered into a partnership with an old friend named Lee. They bought some trade goods, including 100 gallons of booze, and returned to Cheyenne country on the South Platte River. When the Bents learned of his arrival, they assured him that they'd gotten all the furs the Natives had to trade and that his continuing on to trade would make no sense. Jim laughed and soon returned with 400 robes.

"Beckwourth," growled Bent, "how you manage Indians as you do beats my understanding."

"It's easily accounted for," replied Jim. "The Indians know that the whites cheat them, and they know that they can believe what I tell them. Besides that, they naturally feel a superior confidence in me on account of my supposed affinity of race. I have lived so much among them that I can enter into their feelings and be in every respect one of them. It's an inducement that no white trader could ever hope to hold out," he added.

Jim pocketed his profits and returned to Taos, where he set up store and soon married a senorita named Louisa Sandoval. By the fall of 1842, he had partnered with a few other trappers to establish a trading post called Pueblo in present-day Colorado on the Arkansas River. It was a rough place that attracted a collection of shadowy characters. Jim was not immune to the violence that came with them. Old Bill Williams called him a "low-down half-breed nigger Frenchman," and Jim charged him with a knife. Old Bill managed to knock Jim out, and Bill likely fled soon after. It wasn't so much the violence, because he could take care of himself, but the powerful Bent brothers were making it difficult for independent traders. He could make a living in more hospitable places, so Jim turned his eyes west.

In early 1844, Jim arrived at the small Mexican settlement of Pueblo de Los Angeles in present-day California, where he prospered as a trader for a few months. His job brought him into regular contact with the locals, from whom he heard plenty of grumbling about corrupt Mexican officials. Jim came to share the commonly held opinion that President Santa Anna's distant government was interested in the region only for the taxes that could be taken from it, and that the local governor Manuel Micheltorena was a tyrant. Jim joined in the 1845 Californian revolution against Mexican control and fought in the Battle of Cahuenga.

In the spring of 1846, the United States and Mexico went to war over northern Mexican territory. When American soldiers took control of Santa Fe, Jim found work there as an army guide, interpreter and express rider. After charges that he supplemented his income by selling stolen army horses, Jim resigned in anger and returned to Pueblo. There he discovered that his wife had remarried. He left her and his young daughter, headed back to Santa Fe and joined with a partner to buy a hotel. Jim sold out by 1847 and again took odd jobs for the army, operating mostly between Fort Leavenworth, Santa Fe and various places in California.

When gold was discovered east of Sacramento at Sutter's Mill in the spring of 1848, news of it attracted plenty of men looking to make quick and easy fortunes. Some of them were more comfortable using guns and knives than picks and shovels.

James Beckwourth in his 60s, a few years before he met his mysterious end at a Crow camp in 1866

Jim learned that lesson firsthand in late 1848 travelling from Monterey to Nipomo. He was familiar with the route and had made a habit of resting at the Mission San Miguel, owned by William Reed and occupied by his large family.

On this occasion, Jim rode up to the house, slipped off his horse and tied it to a hitching post without receiving a greeting from anyone inside. There was nothing strange there; it was dusk, and he figured the family was eating dinner. He entered the house and called a welcome, but no one answered. His curiosity piqued, Jim wandered through the house. When he reached the kitchen, he saw someone lying on the floor. Jim chuckled, thinking him asleep. He attempted to rouse the man with his foot, but he didn't move. Jim became concerned because of rumors that Natives were raiding in the area, and he suspected that they had attacked those in the house.

Jim ran back to his horse to retrieve his pistols. He returned to the house, lit a candle and began to search the dwelling in earnest. He found the bodies of two women in the first two rooms he entered. Rattled, Jim decided to go for help. Later that evening, he returned to the mission with a posse, and they discovered the 11 bodies of the Reed family and their servants piled high. They searched the house and found the smoldering remains of a failed fire. The grisly mound of bodies was meant to be a pyre.

Jim claimed that he led the posse in pursuit of the murderers. The prominent General William T. Sherman, at that time a lieutenant serving in California, noted that Beckwourth merely reported the incident to him, and that it was the army that pursued and punished the outlaws. Either way, the murderers—white men as it turned out—were hanged. Before one of the outlaws swung, he revealed that his gang had been in the house when Jim was searching it. He informed Jim that he was a lucky man. If he'd gone one room deeper into the building instead of turning for help, he'd have been body number 12.

Jim continued his army work for another few months, but early in 1849, he was caught up in the gold rush that transformed California. In February, he boarded the steamship *California* in Monterey, headed north to Stockton and eventually inland to Sonora. He figured on making his money as a trader, and he brought with him a supply of clothing. He enjoyed enough success to build a small store that he kept supplied with goods from Stockton. However, he soon tired of the inactivity, sold his share in the store to a partner and made for Sacramento. Jim accumulated a small fortune dealing Spanish monte, an easy feat given his skill at the game. And he wasn't tight with his winnings. Jim tossed pouches of gold on the roughly hewn planks that served as tables in the drinking holes with the indifference and pleasure of a prospector who had struck the mother lode.

Jim moved up the American River and wintered with his friend at Murderer's Bar. In 1850 he even tried his hand at prospecting in the American Valley and Pit River country, but the effort was short-lived mostly because of a fortuitous discovery. Jim stumbled on a pass through the northwestern Sierra Nevada Range, a beautiful valley, colorful with vegetation and musical with the sound of birds. From first sight, Jim realized that it was the best route into the American Valley from the east, and he immediately set about laying out a wagon road. The potential was there for good money in such an enterprise. If the route became popular with prospectors and immigrants, then any establishments built on it were likely to fatten the wallets of their owners.

Jim's first challenge was to find investors to bankroll the undertaking. He found civic officials and businessmen in Marysville, California, the western terminus of his proposed road, most interested. They guaranteed the expenses of Beckwourth and Company until the road was passable. The first party finished the journey through the Beckwourth Pass and along the Beckwourth Trail in August 1851. The day after the party arrived in Marysville, town council introduced a motion to remunerate Jim for his expenses. Unfortunately, Marysville suffered two fires in quick succession, and Jim's expenses were the last things on anyone's mind. As late as 1856, Jim was still trying to wring money from the town council, but all he got were reasons it wouldn't be forthcoming.

The enterprise, however, was far from a disaster for Beckwourth. In the spring of 1852 he opened a hotel and store at
the mouth of Big Grizzly Creek near the pass, and although the
number of travelers who used the Beckwourth Trail were not as
high as he'd hoped, he did well enough. A small community
sprang up around Jim's trading post, and he found that he was
a celebrity to passersby. His status was possibly a result of the
publication of his autobiography in 1856 and his willingness
to share a story, often an exaggerated one, with eager listeners.

But by early winter of 1858, Jim was no longer spinning
entertaining yarns at the idyllic setting of Beckwourth Pass. He
left, and no one knows exactly why. Rumors hinted that the size
of his horse herd was less a result of trading than it was of old
horse-thieving habits. Some thought that the law, and more
troublesome, aggrieved settlers were after him. Others thought
that his run of gambling luck had finally run out and that he
was flat broke. Or, it might simply have been that Jim's feet
started itching again. In August 1859, he was back in St. Louis.

Jim wasn't comfortable in the city and complained in good
humor to friends that it had changed so much since his last
visit that he needed a guide while there. He moved around
Missouri, eventually running into his old friend Louis Vasquez,
who offered him a job as an agent-trader at his store in Denver.
Jim accepted, and before year's end, was working with Louis'
nephew at A.P. Vasquez and Company. His appearance in Denver was a matter of public interest, and local newspapers carried stories about him.

The *Rocky Mountain News* confessed, "We had formed the
opinion, as has, we presume, almost everyone, that Captain
Beckwourth was a rough, illiterate, backwoodsman, but were
most agreeably surprised to find him a polished gentleman,
possessing a fund of general information which few can boast."

Jim took a liking to Denver. He bought some land, and
at 60 years of age, eased into the relaxed life of storekeeping.

A real joy was that his business brought him back into contact with the local Natives, but he was disappointed to see the treatment they received from the settlers. He voiced his indignation in a long letter to the *Rocky Mountain News*. On one occasion, Jim went to a camp of Cheyenne and Apache and witnessed grave injustices committed against the Natives:

> *After dark a lot of drunken devils and "bummers" went to the lodges, took the Indian women and girls forcibly out, committing acts of violence, which in any other country would condemn the perpetrators to ignominy and shame. The same night three mules were stolen from the Indians. Indians are as keenly sensible to acts of injustice as they are tenacious of revenge, and it is more humiliating to them to be recipients of such treatments upon their own lands, which they have been deprived of, their game driven off and they made to suffer by hunger, and when they pay a visit, abused more than dogs.*

A public meeting was called to address the injustices done to the Natives and possible remedies. Jim's suggestion was for a municipal law be passed prohibiting the sale of liquor to Natives. His proactive stance resulted in his appointment as the local agent responsible for the Natives during their visits to town. Jim took to the job with enthusiasm. He reported depredations and published notices that the selling of booze to Natives would result in punishment. Locals were so impressed by his work that they proposed contacting officials in Washington in an effort to make Jim the stationary Indian agent. Jim declined, declaring that he wasn't interested in politics.

Jim married again in 1860, but it didn't last long. By 1864 he was living just north of Denver along the South Platte River with a Crow woman, working as a farmer, a trapper and occasionally as a guide for the Colorado Second Infantry.

Jim ran into some trouble with the law. In 1864, he was charged with manslaughter in the death of William "Nigger Bill" Payne, a local blacksmith. The court found that he had indeed killed Payne, but concluded that it was in self-defense. Because Jim was popular in Denver, many celebrated his freedom with him.

Relieved, Jim hurried back to his wife and their small farm, eager for some peace and quiet. He wasn't there long when Colonel George Shoup of the Third Regiment of Colorado Volunteer Cavalry came calling. Jim knew what he was doing there before the officer even spoke. The citizens of Colorado were terrified by the Cheyenne-Arapaho War that had erupted earlier in 1864. Although the local Cheyenne had remained peaceful, Colorado governor John Evans had established the Third Regiment to protect the residents of Denver. Colonel John Chivington commanded the soldiers and directed them to kill Natives on sight, a policy that Governor Evans supported. Shoup informed Jim that his services as a guide were required.

Jim realized that the Natives would inevitably lose control of their country to the United States, but he didn't support war as the best way of going about it.

"If it is the policy of the United States to utterly exterminate the Indian race, the most expeditious manner of effecting this ought to be adopted," he suggested. "The most direct and speedy mode of clearing the land of them would be by the simple means of starvation—by depriving them of their hereditary sustenance, the buffalo. To effect this end, send an army of hunters among them to root out and destroy, in every manner possible, the animal in question."

Perhaps Jim thought that killing the buffalo was less bloody than killing the Natives—more compassionate certainly. Jim's good relationship with the Cheyenne was another reason he didn't want to fight them, but he feared that he might be arrested and killed if he refused Shoup.

Daguerreotype of James Beckwourth, age 55, a year before his popular autobiography was published in 1856

As it happened, Jim was one of the scouts who led Chivington's men to Sand Creek where Black Kettle's band of Cheyenne were camped. Chivington knew that the band was peaceful, but he declared that he had "come to kill Indians, and believe it is right and honorable to use any means under God's heaven to kill Indians." The result was the annihilation of the band in what became known as the Sand Creek Massacre. The scalps of many of the dead Natives were later displayed in Denver, where Chivington was fêted as a hero. But as news of the attack spread, most Americans were outraged, and public pressure resulted in a congressional investigation. Jim was one of many whose testimony revealed the grisly

horror of the affair. The investigation was damning, and faced
with a court-martial, Chivington resigned. A few months after
the incident, Jim visited the Cheyenne and tried to reconcile
with them. When he advised them that the size of the white
population suggested that surrender was their best option, they
told him to leave.

Disheartened, Jim headed back to the woods where he felt
at home. He spent the winter trapping with four partners.
When the ice broke in the spring, the men packed up their furs
and made for Denver. On the way, Blackfoot warriors killed
three of them, and the fourth later drowned in the Green River.
Jim must have reflected on the trials of the previous six years,
and although he wasn't a superstitious man, even he realized
that the foothills of the Rocky Mountains were nothing but
trouble. It was best to move on.

In the summer of 1866, Jim worked as an army scout and
guide at Forts Laramie, Phil Kearny and C.F. Smith along the
Bozeman Trail. It was dangerous work because the Sioux chief
Red Cloud was leading his people in a violent war against
those who used the trail, which cut through the Sioux hunting
grounds of the Powder River country. But the work had its bene-
fits. It brought Jim back into contact with old friends, including
Jim Bridger, who was similarly employed. Their reacquaintance
was brief. In September, Jim traveled north into Crow territory
to hunt. While there he visited a band and fell ill in their camp.
Some claim that he was poisoned in retaliation for allegedly
bringing smallpox to the Crow decades before. He died in Iron
Bull's lodge.

CHAPTER FIVE

Peter Skene Ogden
1794–1854

PETER SKENE OGDEN WAS BORN in 1794 into a family that had lived through remarkable adventures even for the time. His father, Isaac, had been a prominent lawyer in Newark, New Jersey, and his mother, Sarah (Hansen), belonged to the propertied class of that state. The Ogdens supported the British Loyalist Party during the American Revolution, and expectations of victory were great when they moved to New York in 1776. As the tide of the war turned, they were forced to flee to England in 1783. But their love for North America and the tales of western exploration that captivated Isaac made the Ogdens want to return. The opportunity came in 1788 when George III appointed Isaac judge of the Admiralty Court at Québec. They were living in Québec City when Peter was born, the last of nine children.

Isaac Ogden was appointed Judge of the Puisne Court at Montréal soon after Peter's birth, and the burgeoning city on the St. Lawrence furnished the setting for his childhood. Isaac wanted his son to follow him in the law and so provided Peter with a tutor. Peter was not interested in his studies but preferred

North West Company House on Vaudreuil Street in Montréal, where John Jacob Astor lived about 1790

to listen to his father's stories of the western adventures of Peter Pond, explorer and trader. (He didn't know until many years later that Pond was his Christian namesake.) Peter took an equal interest in his mother's accounts of her uncles, of how the family had given the independent-minded young men canoes filled with goods and sent them northwest to trade with the Natives. It was with some pride that Sarah recalled that they had returned as men. But most of all, Peter was captivated by the two-story mansion on the edge of town, the Beaver Lodge.

Everyone in Montréal knew about the Beaver Lodge, an exclusive men's club that was the foundation of the city's aristocracy. It was the headquarters of the North West Company (NWC), a fur-trading organization that took form in the late 1770s. Controlled by Scottish immigrants, the NWC challenged the dominant and longer-established Hudson's Bay Company (HBC). Rather than encourage the Natives to bring their furs to company posts to trade, as was the practice of the HBC, the NWC sent its traders to the Native villages to obtain furs. Canoe brigades, powered by French Canadien *voyageurs*, funneled the furs from the cold north and distant west back to Fort William on Lake Superior and eventually to Montréal. The NWC enjoyed quick and great success, and by the mid-1790s, it controlled two-thirds of the lucrative British North American fur trade.

The interior of the Beaver Lodge resembled a medieval castle, and its lords were the heroes of the fur trade—men like McTavish, Mackenzie, Frobisher and the McGillivrays. Few Montréallers got to see the great banquet hall or enjoy the elaborate ceremonies held in it because membership was limited to those who had spent a winter trading in the northwest. Occasionally, Peter's father and eldest brother were guests, but they were usually ushered out before the celebrations hit full stride late in the evening. Still, the pair had stories enough to intoxicate young Peter, tales of discovery, battles and Natives, tales that time and whiskey had rubbed smooth the sharp edges of deprivation and danger.

Even cautionary tales would not have deterred Peter. He was still a teenager when he informed his parents that he preferred to enter the fur trade rather than train to be a lawyer. They agreed, and Peter got his first job as a clerk, working not for the NWC, which had no positions available, but for the great American fur trader John Jacob Astor. He had little adventure, however, because he spent his days counting furs in Astor's American Fur Company Montréal warehouse. That soon changed. In April 1810, William McGillivray of the NWC offered him a clerkship at £15 a year. Peter was ordered to be ready to leave on May 1 for the 3000-mile journey to the fort at Île à la Crosse.

The journey, taken in large 36-foot canoes across lakes and rivers with occasional portages, took almost three months. Peter was oblivious to the journey's beginnings. While preparing to leave from the great NWC house at Lachine, he had overdone his celebration and passed out drunk. When he awoke, he was in one of the canoes headed up the Ottawa River. His head was still foggy when the paddling *voyageurs* pointed to a large rock in the river.

"Have you ever passed *la roche*?" Jacques asked Peter.

"No, it's my first time," admitted Peter.

"Ahh," nodded Jacques. "Then, there is the matter of a baptism. When one passes *la roche*, he must be baptized."

The others shouted their agreement, and Peter had a chilling vision of a dunk in the cold river. Jacques smiled at the sight of the young man's suddenly wide eyes.

"Perhaps M'sieu Ogden does not like the water? Then we might all share in a baptism of the spirit," he suggested, as he looked to Peter's traveling case.

Peter understood and opened the case. He withdrew one bottle of whiskey, took a last glance at the water and smiled as he popped the cork. He sent the bottle the length of the canoe, and the last man threw the empty container overboard. Laughing, the *voyageurs* broke into a rousing chorus of *La claire fontaine*.

Peter spent a week at Fort William marking fur bales before he continued on with *les hommes du nord*, the *voyageurs* who wintered in the northwest. They arrived at Lac la Crosse as summer's colors were fading and were greeted by a booming cannon from inside the palisades of the fort. Peter was as intrigued by the Cree and Chippewa lodges scattered outside the fort as he was pleased by the comfort of the buildings within. He quickly made friends with Samuel Black, a clerk 10 years his senior, who was free with words of advice and a willing model of appropriate behavior.

"You've taken note of the fort on the far peninsula?" asked Samuel.

"Aye," replied Peter, who knew it to be a HBC post.

"Our job is to mark and count furs," said Samuel. "But our joy is to make life miserable for those bastards. I don't suppose we'll ever force them to move on, but we can make damn well sure they wish they could!"

Peter harassed with gusto. In late October, Peter Fidler, post-master at the local HBC post and well respected within the company, reported a visit by Peter and Samuel. The pair arrived armed, and when they began hurling insults at HBC employees, Fidler ordered them removed. To emphasize his demand, he used a stick to hit Samuel across the arm with such force that the stick snapped.

Although well outnumbered, the NWC men would not be intimidated. Peter drew his dagger and lunged at Fidler to answer the blow. Fidler's heavy coat took the worst of the attack, but one of the jabs drew blood. Samuel took the opportunity to retrieve the broken stick, which he brought crashing down on Fidler's thumb, smashing the nail. Peter found a second stick and added another blow for good measure.

The HBC men, well accustomed to the acrimony that existed between the competing fur companies, stood by in shock at the unexpectedly open and harsh display of violence. Fidler retreated to another room to have his thumb dressed, but Peter and Samuel followed. Peter continued to wield his dagger, and Samuel brandished a pistol. They hurled insults at Fidler, who thought they might attack him again.

Finally, Samuel warned as they left, "You'll not get a single skin at the Île à la Crosse."

North West Company post at Île à la Crosse, 1860. The post was at Lac la Crosse, so named because Natives were playing lacrosse on the island when explorers discovered the lake. When Ogden was stationed there, the fight between the HBC and the NWC for control of the lucrative fur trade was at its bloodiest. His efforts to terrorize employees at an adjacent HBC post were not unusual, although perhaps overly enthusiastic. Ogden's employers were pleased and appointed him master of the company post at nearby Green Lake. But the governors of the HBC did not forget Ogden's brutal harassment. When the fur trading companies merged under the banner of the HBC in 1821, Ogden was denied employment.

Peter added, laughing, "And you'll all have a miserable and unhappy winter!"

Peter wasn't exaggerating. Within a year, Fidler and his men departed, and the NWC traders joyously burned the HBC post to the ground.

Meanwhile, Peter gained a singular reputation for brutality and ruthlessness. While he may have been more zealous in repressing the competition than were other fur traders, his actions were not far out of line for the place and the time. The backdrop was the often-bloody struggle between the NWC and the HBC for control of the lucrative fur trade, and violence was never out of place in the pursuit of the beaver empire. Reports of Peter's activities angered senior officials with the HBC, but his own employers were pleased with his efforts and appointed him master of the company post at Green Lake.

At Green Lake he continued to harass HBC employees, threatening any he encountered with injury and confiscation of goods. In the spring of 1815, a representative of the HBC, which, by its 17th-century charter from the English crown, was the law in Rupert's Land, arrested Peter. He was released before formal charges were laid because the witnesses against him were scattered too far across the northwest to make a trial feasible. The episode did not lessen Peter's appetite for violence. In the spring of the following year, he killed a Native who refused Peter's demand to trade at his NWC post rather than the nearby HBC post. Peter considered his action economically motivated. He didn't dislike Natives; indeed, he had taken one as a wife and would eventually have two children by her. Perhaps it was as much pleasure as commerce that led him to join with Samuel Black in an attack on the Green Lake HBC post in 1817. They stole the competition's furs and escorted the employees back to Île à la Crosse, where they were confined temporarily.

Peter was not troubled by guilt, which he thought had no place in a world ruled by decisive action. He defended his

position to Ross Cox, a fellow NWC employee whom he met at
Île à la Crosse.

"My legal primer says that necessity has no law; and in this
place, where the custom of the country, or as lawyers say, *Lex
non scripta* (the unwritten law) is our only guide, we must in all
our acts of summary legislation sometimes perform the parts
of judge, jury, sheriff, hangman, gallows and all!"

Peter overstated his position because the HBC and not NWC
employees properly exercised legal rights in the fur-trading
territory. Jurisprudence aside, Ross found the master of the
NWC's Green Lake post interesting, describing him as "the
humorous, honest, eccentric, law-defying Peter Ogden, the terror of Indians and the delight of all gay fellows."

Peter's violent ways caught up with him in 1818, when a court
in Lower Canada returned an indictment for murder against
him. HBC authorities arrived at Green Lake to arrest him only
to discover that Peter had gone across the mountains, headed
for the Columbia River, a region then controlled by the NWC,
where British law could not reach him. The untamed character of the Pacific Northwest likely appealed to Peter. Certainly,
his employers believed he had the fortitude to deal with the
dangers of the region. When he arrived at Fort George on the
Columbia River, one of his first assignments was leading a
party into Puget Sound to address the recent murder of an Iroquois trapper associated with the NWC by a Cowlitz Native.
The incident proved disastrous. The Iroquois who accompanied him killed 13 Cowlitz in revenge, and Peter and his party
had to flee. To reconcile with the Cowlitz and preserve a tat-
tered trading relationship, Peter married the daughter of the
chief.

In the spring of 1820, Peter was assigned to take charge of
the Shuswap District to the north of the Columbia River. He
was stationed at Fort Thompson, New Caledonia. Peter continued to prove his value as an employee, and in the fall, he

received notice that he had been given one share in the NWC. Peter was finally a partner! But the news proved bittersweet. Just one year later, in the summer of 1821, the fur war between the NWC and the HBC came to an end, with the HBC staggering to victory. The companies were to unite, but Peter was informed that the reorganized HBC did not require his services. He was one of three men, including his old friend Samuel Black, who was unacceptable to the governors of the company. His violent past had taken its toll, and it appeared as if Peter's fur-trading days were a thing of the past.

But Peter had supporters among the local chief factors (those in charge of HBC fur-trading posts). And while the new governor of the HBC's North American holdings, George Simpson, was far too autocratic to listen to the advice of those who served under him, he realized that winter was approaching and that no one was in position to take command of Fort Thompson. Simpson, who was charged with reversing the HBC's economic slide, also harbored a suspicion that Ogden might go to the Columbia to compete as an independent fur trader and thus interfere with the company's bottom line. He asked Peter to remain at Fort Thompson for the winter, after which a decision regarding his employment would be made.

Peter agreed to stay, but he was not willing to wait and let others decide his fate. In the spring of 1822, he set out for London to attend a meeting with the Board of the HBC, determined to press his case. In early 1823 in London, he was surprised to find William McGillivray, his old NWC employer. McGillivray had been appointed a senior member of the HBC and was in London for the company's winter meetings. While there, he had spoken for Ogden and Black. McGillivray assured Peter that he would have a place in the HBC. In late February, Peter received word that he and Samuel were appointed clerks of the first class, each with a chief trader's salary. Furthermore, Peter would be appointed a chief trader later that year.

It was a great victory for Peter, a statement of the company's regard for his ability. When he returned to British North America that summer, he was given command of the Spokane District, an unheard-of assignment for one who was only 29. He arrived at Spokane House in late October. The journey had been a difficult one, during which Peter suffered from malaria. He took time to recover, and that was not difficult in the pleasant atmosphere of the well-stocked post. The presence of Native women added to the men's comfort, and Peter was among those interested in their companionship. His previous two wives had moved on, and while he wasn't looking to take a wife, he knew that such a relationship would strengthen trading bonds between the fort and the local Natives.

Peter was drawn to Julia Rivet, a Flathead whose stepfather was Francois Rivet, an interpreter with the HBC who had accompanied Lewis and Clark on their western expedition. Julia was different from many of the Native women at the fort. She appeared only occasionally and refused to dress in the European costumes popular among many of the others. But she danced at the balls, and Peter looked forward to spins around the floor. He found Julia's frankness in conversation especially appealing. Peter was smitten, and he headed off for the Flathead camp to follow up his interest. Julia was unresponsive and uninterested in a casual relationship. Peter was persistent and returned many times, but Julia remained equally obstinate. Finally, Peter proposed marriage, but it was not until he'd spent half his savings on 50 horses for Julia's mother in the Flathead marriage rite that Julia consented to be his wife. The ceremony was completed by a ride around the Flathead camp. Peter sent for his children who were at Fort Île à la Crosse, and the family, save for children yet to come, was complete.

Peter did not remain long at Spokane House. In the summer of 1824, George Simpson directed him to the Columbia

Daguerreotype of Ogden, age 28, likely made in England, where he traveled in 1822 to press his case for employment with the HBC

District, then under the command of Dr. John McLoughlin. In his efforts to improve HBC profits, Simpson turned his eye to the basin of the Snake River, which is the great tributary of the Columbia River. The HBC had sent expeditions to Snake country before, so Simpson knew beaver was plentiful, but he was also eager to stop American expansion into the northwest. Ownership of the region remained in dispute because Britain and the United States could not agree on a boundary linking the Rocky Mountains and the Pacific coast. Since an 1818 convention of agreement, the two countries had shared the region. Everyone knew that the awkward situation could not continue indefinitely, and most expected that the nation with the most citizens in the region would ultimately control it. Simpson wanted his company's employees to go into Snake country, trap it clean and thereby remove the incentive for American trappers to come to the Pacific Northwest.

Previous HBC Snake country expeditions had not been successful, which Simpson thought reflected poor planning. Simpson proposed that the next expedition would leave in the fall, winter in the south and trap the prime winter beaver as they returned north. It was not a desirable assignment because no one wanted to suffer through the winter in exposed conditions. Simpson turned to Ogden, who shared the general apathy about the mission, but Simpson sweetened the assignment by appointing Peter as chief trader before the expedition set off.

Peter arrived at Flathead Post on Clark's (Clark) Fork, the jumping off point, in early November and began preparing for the expedition. He hired freemen—independent trappers who traded their furs to the HBC—to accompany the HBC engagés (employees). The freemen were valuable to any expedition because they were not an expense to the HBC, and they were actually at the mercy of the HBC because the company set trading prices in the isolated west. While the HBC was eager to keep the freemen content because of their importance in acquiring furs, with the competition necessary to ensure fair value for pelts, the freemen were often underpaid. As a result, they could be unreliable. The danger lay with Americans trying to pry away freemen with better offers for their furs or with encouragement to desert. And Peter knew that American traders were in the region. While at Flathead Post, he met with

Alexander Ross who had just returned from the Snake country. With him were seven American trappers employed by William Ashley and Andrew Henry, including Jedidiah Smith. Peter was likely upset. Ross had orders not to assist any Americans, and yet he had brought them back to HBC territory! They wouldn't be there for long. When Peter left on December 20, 1824, the Americans followed him.

At Julia's insistence Peter's family was among the 22 lodges of the expedition, which included 10 engagés and 53 freemen. Patterns that characterized the expedition emerged early. They encountered Natives and so required extra guards to protect the horses. The matter became more serious early in the new year, when they reached the country of the hostile Blackfoot. Not only did the Blackfoot steal horses, they were also known to kill intruders into their territory. In addition, the weather was soon numbingly cold, and the snow was thick and often impassable, sometimes forcing the party to retrace hard-won steps to seek alternative routes.

In mid-January, the party slipped through Gibbon's Pass in the Bitterroot Mountains, crossing the continental divide. They trapped south of the mountains, and by late March, crossed the Snake Plain. In late April, Peter recorded that the party's beaver count reached 1000. But problems awaited on the horizon.

On May 22, as the expedition camped near the Bear River, a party of American trappers arrived. Peter hoped there would be no trouble, as was the case when Jedidiah Smith's men rode with them in the spring. When the Americans set up camp nearby, Peter discovered that tranquility was not to be had. The Americans' leader, Johnson Gardner, encouraged the HBC freemen and engagés to desert. Peter was concerned because some deserters from previous HBC expeditions were among the Americans. More worrisome, however, were Gardner's brash pronouncements.

"Do you know whose country you are in?" barked Johnson.

"I do not," replied Peter. "It has not been determined between Britain and America to whom it belongs."

"You're mistaken," smiled Johnson smugly. "The matter has been decided, and the territory has been ceded to America. And you do not have license to trap or trade here, so you'd best return north."

There had been no such agreement made, and unbeknownst to both Ogden and Gardner, they were actually in Mexican territory!

"Our return shall only be dictated by orders from the British government," declared Peter. "Without such orders, we will remain."

"Then you remain at your peril," snarled Johnson, as he left the tent.

Peter followed him outside and watched him go to John Grey's tent. Grey was a freeman and long considered a troublemaker by Peter and others in the HBC hierarchy. Peter walked over to the tent.

"You have had these men already too long in your service, Mr. Ogden," accused Johnson. "You have most shamefully imposed on them, selling them goods at high prices and giving them nothing for their skins."

Grey nodded in agreement.

"Those who operate the HBC posts on the Columbia are the greatest villains in the world," John added. "I admit that you have been fair to me and the others, but many of the freemen have long wished for an opportunity to join the Americans. We are now in a free country with friends to help us," he said, as he placed his hand on Johnson's shoulder. "Now, we will go, and nothing you can say will prevent us."

John stepped out of the tent and told the others to prepare to leave. Some of the Americans approached the camp with their rifles leveled to offer protection. Eleven men left, but Peter successfully prevented them from stealing the party's horses.

Peter heaved a sigh of relief when the Americans struck camp. Still, he remained worried that more freemen might join them. The next day it was rumored that the Americans were going to attack. Peter ordered a strict guard, and while the Americans returned, they left without violence, but with more freemen and an additional warning from Johnson.

"If you do not leave willingly, our troops will arrive this fall to force you to do so."

Peter was concerned, but could do nothing but begin the return journey north to the Columbia River. In mid-July, he sent Kittson ahead to Flathead Post with 20 packhorses loaded with pelts. When he finally reached Fort Nez Perces (on a tributary of the Columbia River) in early November, his command was reduced to 16 men, who required the protection of friendly Flathead for the last month of their journey. All was not lost, however, because the expedition netted 4000 pelts, which was more than Ross had brought in the year before.

George Simpson was pleased with the returns; not only would the furs taken by the Snake Country Expedition improve HBC profits, they were also kept out of American hands. He ordered Ogden to return south, this time to trap the territory west and south of the Snake River. Following an unexpected, but brief reunion with Samuel Black, who had recently been appointed chief trader at Fort Nez Perces, Peter's expedition set out on November 20, 1825.

Despite Julia's protests, she was not allowed to accompany the party. No women were to accompany them, perhaps to save on food, although many of the wives and companions of the traders stealthily joined the party some days later. Perhaps they later wished they hadn't; the winter proved most difficult. The weather often kept them stalled in camp, and the territory was barren of game.

They were forced to kill horses for food. And still no beaver! Peter soon learned why the streams were barren. Snake braves informed him that the local Natives had been trapping in hopes of deterring white trappers from entering the region. They were using the HBC strategy! Peter was likely too miserable to see the irony in it. His party's luck changed in mid-March, soon after they reached the Snake River. A friendly Snake agreed to join them as a guide, and almost immediately the hunters brought down 13 elk. Their bellies full, the men were able to focus on trapping once more. It was none too soon.

In late March came word that Americans were trapping within three day's journey. Peter was worried. The harshness of the winter had him concerned that the men would be all too anxious to desert given an opportunity. On April 9, the Americans stumbled into camp and with them several deserters from the previous year.

"If we were surprised at seeing them," said Peter, "they were more so at seeing us from an idea that their threats of last year would have prevented me from again returning to this quarter, but they find themselves mistaken."

Peter also felt a measure of relief at the arrival of the Americans. They had seen Blackfoot braves in the past week, and Peter was certain that they would be less willing to attack a larger group of trappers. Still, he would not let the Americans camp too close to his party. The next day they appeared at camp and offered to trade their furs to Peter. He realized that his concern was undue. From what Peter observed, the deserters had already tired of their American masters, and he thought they would soon return. When the Americans departed without any additional deserters, two remained with Peter's party.

The willingness of the men to remain with the HBC expedition did not mean they were pleased with their situation. By mid-May, they were clamoring to return to Fort Nez Perces. Peter could hardly blame them. Many had no shoes, and even though they were quite used to suffering, two-thirds of them had no blankets or any shelter for the past six months. Perhaps

Fort Vancouver at the mouth of the Columbia River, 1853. Ogden was chief factor at the former HBC fort in the Pacific Northwest.

Peter shared their desire to return when he fell sick from poisoned beaver a week later. But his duty to the company came first, and by mid-June they had taken 2000 beaver. When they finally arrived at the recently constructed Fort Vancouver on the Columbia River on July 17, they had with them 3800 pelts.

Peter found Julia waiting there with their new daughter Sarah, but he had little time to relax. On September 11, 1826, he departed on his third Snake Country Expedition. They traveled west of the Snake River, south to the Klamath region. Within weeks, the Snake were stealing expedition goods and horses. In early October, on the Crooked River, the Natives launched their boldest attack. Under cover of darkness, they slipped across the river and set fire to the grass a short 10 yards from the camp, and only a break of willows prevented its complete destruction. Peter was livid; the Snake had recently been in camp and were well fed there.

Angry as Peter was, he knew that most of the Natives in the Snake country, save the Blackfoot, could be counted on to trade furs and food. More than once, a supply of their salmon or meat had saved the trappers from starvation. But the Natives encountered on this journey were in desperate straits. Peter did not realize the extent of their plight until an encounter with an old Native woman in late October. He wrote in his journal:

> From the severe weather last year, her people were reduced from want of food to subsist on the bodies of relations and children. She herself had not killed any but had fed on two of her own children who died thro' weakness.... What an example to us at present reduced to one meal a day, how loudly and grievously we complain; when I consider the Snake sufferings compared to our own. Many a day they pass without food and without a murmur.

Soon the trappers' situation approached the grimness of the Snake River. In early November, the men had eaten only six meals in 10 days. By late November, they were eating horses, and soon, dogs. Beaver could have filled empty stomachs, but the traps were always empty. By December, Peter was losing faith.

What will become of us? he wrote despairingly in his journal.

On New Year's Day, 1827, he tried to lift spirits by dispersing tobacco and liquor to the men.

Early February found the men in northeastern California. They discovered a prominent peak, and Peter named it Mt. Shastise (Mt. Shasta). For a few weeks, they were busy trapping beaver, but by mid-March the desperation that had characterized so much of the journey reasserted itself.

Peter wrote in his journal,

> *All obliged to camp out in pouring rain without blankets. Not one complaint. This life makes a young man sixty in a few years....A convict at Botany Bay is a gentleman at ease compared to my trappers.*

By late May, Peter was convinced that the expedition would lose money. It almost proved more costly than that. In June, Peter fell ill. The tribulations of the journey—the cold weather, lack of food, long hours and stress of leadership—and the contaminated water of Malheur Lake kept him in bed for 10 days. Fortunately, Julia was there to minister to him, and Peter recovered. On August 5, the party finally reached Fort Vancouver, but they had little opportunity to either rest or relax. On August 24, Peter left Fort Vancouver for Fort Nez Perces, where he visited briefly with his old friend Black. On September 7, 1827, Peter made his way back to the Snake country for the fourth time. For the most part, the expedition was to stay north of the Snake River, except for their return, which hugged the river's southern shoreline.

The HBC men would have company for much of this expedition. In late September, they encountered American trappers led by John Johnson near Wayer's River (Weiser River). They informed Peter that other Americans were trapping in the region. Peter cursed the news. Surely it would mean fewer beaver for his own party. The Americans, short on supplies, joined the expedition as freemen. Peter was pleased with the arrangement since it reduced the competition. Peter later discovered that his concerns about the Americans were once again overstated because the five men, who were near to starving when they joined Peter, did not make any attempt to trap beaver. They gambled their days away and left the trapping to Peter's men. Although these were not the only Americans Peter encountered on his journey, none of them caused any problems for the HBC trappers.

Julia gave birth to a son in February 1828, but the infant died in March. It was not the only death on the expedition. In late May, on the Black Feet (Blackfoot) River, Blackfoot warriors killed a trapper. Peter was philosophical about the loss of life. It was distressing and regrettable, but he had learned that such things happened no matter what precautions were taken to prevent them.

The men returned to Fort Nez Perces on July 22. They had trapped more than 3000 beavers, and the expedition was considered a success. The returns far exceeded Peter's expectations and were sufficient to convince George Simpson that another expedition was warranted. On September 22, 1828, Peter set off on his fifth journey into the Snake country. With him were Julia and their five children. The expedition took Peter farther south than he had been before, to the Humboldt River (he discovered and named it) and north of the Great Salt Lake.

In early November near the Great Salt Lake, the party encountered Natives who had probably not seen white men before. Peter detained them in hopes of securing information, but they could not communicate and fled when released. An encounter with the Modoc Natives along the Humboldt River in mid-May proved more hair-raising for the HBC men. Peter had divided his party into three groups so he had only 12 men with him when a party of 200 Natives approached his camp. Peter believed that these Modoc were the war party responsible for a recent attack on one of his trappers, which also saw the loss of some traps and horses. Peter feared the worst but did not reveal it. Instead, he had his Snake guide set up a parley with the Modoc leaders. During the meeting, Peter noticed that the Modoc had various items that he suspected were stolen from Jedidiah Smith's trapping party, which was almost wiped out on the Umpqua River in July 1828. The Modoc did not attack the HBC party. Respecting Peter's courage and goodwill, the Natives gave him information about the region, and early the next morning, Peter struck camp and left.

The fifth Snake Country Expedition ended on July 8 when the party returned to Fort Nez Perces. The returns again far exceeded Peter's expectations, approximately 4000 beaver. George Simpson was most impressed by Peter's efforts, as he stated in a letter to the Governors and Committee of the Hudson's Bay Company in London:

> *I cannot quit the subject of our trapping expeditions, without expressing my utmost satisfaction with the zeal, activity and perseverance manifested by Chief Trader Ogden in the very arduous service on which he has been employed for some years past; while I am sorry to intimate, that the injury his constitution has sustained, by the privations and discomfort to which he has been so long exposed, will render it necessary to relieve him as soon as we can find a gentleman qualified to fill his place to advantage.*

An able replacement was not found before the sixth Snake Country Expedition was ready to depart, so Peter again led the brigade. He first saw his eldest son, also named Peter, off to school in Red River, then said goodbye to his family, leaving Fort Vancouver in late summer 1829. The expedition trapped farther south than any previous. They traveled along the Gulf of California and the Sierra Mountains and through the San

Joaquin Valley, deep into Mexican territory. However, beyond the loss of nine men and 500 pelts swept away on the Columbia River, little is known of the details of the journey because Peter lost his journal near its completion.

The returns of Peter's sixth expedition were the poorest yet, but he had earned his reward. John Work replaced Peter, and on orders from Simpson he led an expedition to dislodge the Americans from the sea otter trade. The value of that trade had decreased in recent years, but Simpson was less interested in making a profit than he was in asserting economic control over the region. In the fall of 1830, Peter prepared to sail for the Nass River, where he was to build a fort designed to siphon trade from American competitors. But while in Fort Vancouver, he was struck down with malaria. The ensuing epidemic proved tragic, wiping out 75 percent of the local Native population. Peter recovered, and in the spring of 1831, his family boarded the *Cadboro* for the mouth of the Nass River. He selected a suitable site, only accessed by coastal Natives, and oversaw the construction of Fort Simpson, which was completed in August.

Peter remained there until the spring of 1834, when he received notice that he would be leading an expedition to the north up the Stikine River, where he would construct another fort. The post was to be in British territory, but the mouth of the Stikine River was in the Russian territory of Alaska. Baron Wrangell, the governor of Alaska, was not pleased to learn that the HBC was sending Peter north. Wrangell knew something of Peter's successful excursions into the Snake country, and the Russian feared that he might enjoy similar success in Alaska. He was determined to prevent that.

In mid-June, Peter's ship, the *Dryad*, anchored in the Stikine Sound near the Russian post of Point Highfield. A Russian officer came aboard the ship with a document prohibiting British trade in Russian waters.

"It's all fine and good," stated Peter. "But the Hudson's Bay Company has no desire to trade here. We wish only safe passage to British territory as assured by treaty."

The officer threw his hands in the air, mumbled a few words of Russian and left. It was the beginning of a most frustrating month for Peter. He tried to communicate with numerous Russian officials but none spoke English, and he employed no one who spoke Russian.

On one occasion, when Peter declared that the *Dryad* was going upriver, he was told, "No. If you try, the fort will buxom you."

Despite the best efforts of Peter and his officers, no one could figure out what a buxoming implied, but they all agreed that it was best to remain anchored. Finally, Peter visited Point Highfield, where he learned that the Russians were awaiting word from Wrangell at Sitka. His directions arrived in mid-July. The Russians would not allow the *Dryad* to proceed. After discussing the matter with his officers, Peter decided it best not to test the cannon of Point Highfield, and he directed the captain to return to the Nass River. Once there, Peter relocated Fort Simpson because its original location was far too exposed to icy winter gales. The carpenters on the *Dryad* were put to work dismantling the old fort and moving it to a more suitable location, a sheltered bay on the Nass estuary. It was difficult work, completed in about seven weeks by the end of August 1834. Peter's superiors in London were not pleased with the turn of events along the Stikine River, particularly because they had the law on their side. When they pressed Russian officials to cover the expenses of the expedition, the Russians instead chose to allow future vessels to travel unimpeded up the Stikine.

Peter did not remain long on the Nass River. In September 1835, word arrived from London that he had been appointed Chief Factor of the New Caledonia District. It was a good assignment. Headquartered at Fort St. James on Stuart Lake,

Peter was in charge of eight posts. As chief factor, Peter had servants to meet all his needs, including his limited transportation requirements—*voyageurs* carried him on and off boats as necessary! Furthermore, because of his experience and good fortune, Peter established an excellent relationship with the local Carrier Natives. He treated their chief 'Kwah as an equal and attended the Natives' potlatch ceremonies. But Peter also bore an uncanny resemblance to a prominent 17th-century chief, and the Carrier thought Ogden was a reincarnation of the man. Good relations added to the company's bottom line, and in his first year as chief factor, Peter netted a profit of £10,000.

Peter led the annual fur brigade to Fort Vancouver, always making a brief stop at Fort Kamloops to meet with his old friend Samuel Black, who was stationed there in 1830 and subsequently made chief factor of the Thompson River District in 1837. Those happy sojourns came to an end in 1841, when the son of a recently deceased chief killed Samuel. The murder wasn't born of animosity. Samuel was well respected by the Natives, which contributed to his untimely death. The local Natives had a tradition that demanded the death of one of equal standing to the deceased; a chief factor was appropriate. Peter was given charge of Samuel's old Thompson River District.

In the summer of 1844, Peter was granted a one-year vacation. He left his wife and children in Fort Vancouver and returned east to the newly created province of Lower Canada to visit family before sailing to England and the continent. The trip was not a pleasant one, particularly because Peter discovered that a long-standing estrangement with his brother Charles was irreconcilable. He returned to Red River in Rupert's Land in the spring of 1845, where he found waiting an urgent letter from George Simpson. American politicians were debating the future of Oregon Territory, and Peter, one of Simpson's

Daguerreotype of Ogden, age 56, having completed six Snake Country expeditions

most trusted men, was needed back in the Columbia Region to address the situation.

Simpson suggested that the Americans were planning to take the region by possession. They were sending settlers there under the direction of the prominent explorer Lieutenant John Fremont. Simpson knew that the region retained little economic value for its furs, but he wasn't going to let it slip away simply because of American acquisitiveness. Peter was

to guide two lieutenants from Red River to the Pacific Northwest. The pair was to evaluate the situation, map out a route
across the continent for British troops and take title of Cape
Disappointment (on the northern side of the mouth of the
Columbia River) before the Americans arrived. Simpson
made it clear that no land was to be secured by force. If settlers were discovered, their property was to be purchased.
When the party arrived at Cape Disappointment, they had
to do just that.

Peter carried out his obligations without enthusiasm. He
thought that the dispute over the Oregon Territory should be
resolved peacefully. In any case, Simpson's plan was derailed
when Peter discovered that 30 American families, too many to
relocate, were living in the region. Dr. John McLoughlin, chief
factor of the Columbia District, was blamed for their presence.
He accepted the responsibility and defended himself on
humanitarian grounds: the Americans would have starved or
been killed by Natives without HBC support. Simpson
removed McLoughlin from his position and placed the district under the management of a board consisting of Ogden,
James Douglas, and briefly, McLoughlin.

Peter never returned to New Caledonia, but pleasant times
at Fort Vancouver in Oregon Territory eased the separation.
He judged horse races at a local track and served as patron of
the Vancouver Curling Club. At 51, his exploits had earned
respect. But he was also jovial and warm by nature, and his
demeanor contributed to his great popularity. Peter was content to let British and American government officials work
out the long-standing dispute over the Oregon Territory.
Word came in the fall of 1846 that the boundary matter had
been settled. The dividing line was the 49th parallel, south
of President James Polk's desired 54'40", but north of the
Columbia Region. Peter thought that the British could have

made a better deal, especially given the HBC's past efforts in the territory.

In early December 1847, a crisis drew Peter from the relative comfort of Fort Vancouver back into the field. He was enjoying an evening meal when a courier arrived with urgent news. A band of Cayuse had attacked the Methodist mission at Waiilatpu on the Walla Walla River. Dr. Marcus Whitman, the missionary, his wife and 12 others were killed, and 50 more were taken prisoner. While many thought the Whitmans responsible for their own demise, Peter realized that the situation required action rather than blame. He set off with two canoes full of goods to be given as ransom for the captives. En route, he learned that a company of American riflemen had been dispatched from the Williamette Valley to address the situation in frontier style. What was urgent had become grave. Peter knew that if the armed men arrived before he did, there would be no negotiations, and the captives would surely die.

Peter reached Fort Walla Walla on December 19 before the riflemen. He called a council of the Cayuse chiefs, and they agreed to attend. Peter took the initiative.

> *We have been among you for thirty years, without the shedding of blood. We are traders, and of a different nation than the Americans. But, recollect, we supply you with ammunition, not to kill Americans, who are of the same color, speaking the same language and worshipping the same God as ourselves, and whose cruel fate causes our hearts to bleed. Why do we make you chiefs if you cannot control your young men? Besides this wholesale butchery, you have robbed the Americans passing through your country and have insulted their women. If you allow your young men to govern you, I say you are not men or chiefs but she-men who do not deserve the name.*

Your hotheaded young men plume themselves on their bravery; but let them not deceive themselves. If the Americans begin war, they will have cause to repent their rashness, for the war will not end until every man of you is cut off from the face of the earth! I am aware that many of your people have died....You have the opportunity to make some reparation. I give you only advice and promise you nothing, should war be declared against you. The company will have nothing to do with your quarrel.

If you wish it, on my return, I will see what can be done for you; but I do not promise to prevent war. Deliver me the prisoners to return to their friends, and I will pay you a ransom; that is all.

It was enough. Tiloukaikt, a prominent chief, spoke for the Cayuse.

Chief, your words are weighty—your hairs are gray! In life there are ties of blood between us; and in death your Company has allowed our dead to sleep beside yours. We have known you a long time. You have had an unpleasant journey to this place. I cannot, therefore, keep the families back. I make them over to you, which I would not do to another younger than myself.

The captives were returned, for the most part unharmed. But soon afterwards, the Americans attacked the transgressors in what became known as the Cayuse War. By that time, Peter was back at Fort Vancouver.

He received a letter of thanks from Governor George Abernethy of the Oregon Country and modestly replied, "I was the mere acting agent of the Hudson's Bay Company."

As Peter turned 55 in 1849, his responsibilities were again increased. James Douglas was sent north to Fort Victoria to manage the company's new holdings on Vancouver Island, so Peter became the sole chief factor at Fort Vancouver. Business was more tangled than ever. The HBC was operating in a foreign country, which meant duties to pay and political sensitivities to negotiate. Furthermore, the challenges had to be met in a rapidly changing world. The discovery of gold in California in early 1848 soon affected the Columbia Region. Men resigned to prospect, and company profits fell. Peter was forced to face the fact that the fur traders were a doomed race.

Peter fell ill from his recurring bout with malaria in 1851, but by summer's end he had recovered sufficiently for a business trip to the East. In the late fall, he sailed via Panama and landed in New York in January 1852 before traveling to Montréal to visit relatives and then on to Washington. At the direction of HBC officials, he sought compensation for company expenses incurred during the Cayuse War (the HBC had given supplies to the Americans) and sought to sell company holdings in the Columbia Region. Peter met with President Millard Fillmore, who tersely informed him that there would be neither compensation nor purchase. Peter considered the president's response a dishonorable one, but he accepted it in what the local newspapers described as a statesmanlike manner.

Peter remained in eastern British North America through 1852, operating out of Lachine, where he continued to fulfill HBC duties. He set out for home in January 1853, again traveling by way of Panama. On the final leg of the journey, his steamer, the *Tennessee*, ran aground in a fog near San Francisco. Although the Californian city was only four miles north, Peter was not certain when a rescue party would arrive, and he did not relish waiting in the chill, damp winter wind. Unfortunately, he had in his possession a locked valise containing several thousand dollars in gold coin, which he could not carry to San Francisco. So he placed soiled clothes on top of the gold, left the valise unlocked and set off north with 100 other passengers who had also chosen to complete the journey on foot.

When Peter returned to the site of the wrecked *Tennessee* the next day, the makeshift camp was in a shambles. Most of the 500 passengers who had remained were gone, and the belongings that had been left behind had been ransacked. Peter noticed that many locked trunks and cases had been broken open. He finally stumbled upon his valise, some of the soiled clothes within were pulled out and draped over its sides. But inside remained the gold.

Peter finally reached the Columbia River a few weeks later. He remained in charge of Fort Vancouver for a few more months and then moved to a house he had recently purchased in Oregon City. His health continued to fail through 1854. He died peacefully on September 27, 1854, with his wife Julia by his side.

CHAPTER SIX

Jedidiah Smith
1799–1831

NEW ENGLAND WAS HOME to Jedidiah Smith's people for nearly 200 years before his parents looked west. Jedidiah Sr. and Sally Strong left Connecticut and made their way to Jericho (present-day Bainbridge in New York state) in the Susquehanna Valley after the American Revolution had run its course. The Smiths opened a store and did a good business selling to the burgeoning population of settlers. The family was there about nine years when Jedidiah, Jr., was born on January 6, 1799, the sixth of 13 children. The habits that shaped Jedidiah's life were formed in the carefree days of youth in the lush Susquehanna Valley. Beyond the cleared and planted fields was plenty to occupy a boy, and Diah, as the lad was called, explored, hunted and nurtured a love for the outdoors. But Diah's character was shaped as much by his family as by the surrounding wilderness. The Smiths were intimate and God-fearing, and Diah would never forget the importance of either sibling or Maker.

Diah was 12 when his family moved to Erie County, Pennsylvania. It was there that he first dreamed of western adventure. His family became acquainted with the local doctor, Titus Simons, and Diah grew especially close to him. Dr. Simons gave Diah a copy of Lewis and Clark's narrative of their historic journey to the Pacific Ocean. The book had a profound impact on the boy, who is said to have carried it with him on his subsequent western travels. Before he struck out on his own adventures, however, Diah's family moved one last time in 1817 to Ashtabula on the shores of Lake Erie.

In 1821 Diah left his family. He spent time in north Illinois, eventually drifting down to St. Louis, a new frontier spectacle for Diah. St. Louis boasted a population of 5000, many of whom lived in crowded, dirty and busy streets along the Mississippi River. And the river was choked with steamboats, keelboats, canoes and other vessels whose odd structures defied labeling. Beyond and above the cluttered waterfront were stately and well-spaced homes along paved roads. St. Louis was a town of contrasts, where those in fine silks and cottons rubbed elbows with those in buckskin and homespun. Throughout the winter of 1821–22, however, the conversation in parlor rooms and taverns alike swirled around the same topic.

For some time, rumor had it that a trading expedition bound for unknown western lands would be launched from St. Louis. One-time Missouri militia officers General William Ashley, lieutenant-governor of Missouri, and Major Andrew Henry, long-time trapper, were believed to be associated with the undertaking. Rumor became fact on February 13, 1822, when an advertisement detailing the particulars of the expedition appeared in the local *Missouri Gazette & Public Advertiser*.

> *To Enterprising Young Men!*
> *The subscriber wishes to engage 100 men to ascend the river Missouri to its source, there to be employed for one, two or three years. For particulars, inquire of Major Andrew Henry,*

*near the lead mines, in the County of Washington (who will
ascend with and command the party) or to the subscribed at
St. Louis.*
Wm. H. Ashley

Diah, who hadn't enjoyed much luck finding work since
leaving home, saw the advertisement as a welcome opportunity. He met with Ashley and listened as the proprietor
explained the mission in a brief and businesslike fashion.

"The object of the undertaking is to hunt and trap. The
company will engage some 180 young men and transport
them to the Three Forks of the Missouri River, a region that
reports suggest has a wealth of furs not surpassed by the mines
of Peru. Major Henry is already en route with the first contingent of trappers. It will be difficult work," added Ashley, "done
in relative isolation and under challenging conditions. But it's
best you enter it with your eyes wide open."

Diah wasn't put off by a challenge and offered his services to the general. Ashley was taken by the young man, who
was six feet tall with an equal measure of determination. He
hired Diah on the spot as a hunter for the expedition. On
May 8, Diah boarded the keelboat *Enterprize*, under the command of Daniel Moore and headed up the Missouri River to
join Major Henry and his men at the mouth of the Yellowstone River.

Diah didn't have time to get comfortable on the *Enterprize*.
Three weeks out, the keelboat caught a large overhanging tree
and was swept under in a strong current. The vessel and
$10,000 worth of cargo was lost. Moore returned to St. Louis to
take Ashley the bad news. Surely the entrepreneur expected setbacks, but such a costly one so early in the undertaking! Nevertheless, he fitted out another vessel and joined Moore when
it set out. They soon rejoined Diah and the others, and together
they continued north. Gradually, the country changed, and

Jedidiah Smith, possibly drawn by a friend after the mountain
man's death at the hand of Comanche braves in 1831

a new world emerged as they passed the Platte River and the
last of the military forts and fur posts at Council Bluffs to the
north.

The vast prairie especially impressed Diah. It rolled back
from the stands of trees along the river, and as the breeze gently rippled the grass, the prairie appeared as a great green lake.
With his hunter's eye, Diah observed the abundant wildlife,

mostly antelope but also deer, bear and elk. He also took note of the Natives. He saw Kaw and Ponca, but was most impressed with the Sioux, who were as different from the degraded Natives he had seen in the eastern settlements as the jack pine from the oak.

> *The Sioux are generally above the common stature and of a complexion somewhat lighter than most Indians,* he reflected in his journal. *They have intelligent countenances and are in person generally good-looking men. In the moral scale, as their appearance would indicate, they rank above the mass of Indians.*

Diah had good opportunity to take measure of the Sioux during the first months of the expedition. Aware of their strength and the vast territory they controlled, Ashley was careful to avoid the appearance of intrusion and to distribute gifts to them whenever possible.

Travel on the Missouri River continued to prove difficult. The current, stretches of shallow water and tangled underbrush tested the muscles and determination of even the best boatmen. By early September, Ashley and his men reached the Ree (Arikara) villages a few miles above the Grand River. Ashley grew impatient to meet up with Major Henry, so he made plans to abandon the river for a land route. He purchased some horses from the Ree, divided his party and led a small group, including Diah, to the Yellowstone River. They stopped for one day at the Mandan villages near the Little Missouri River, where Ashley took a short break to attend a council and to curry their favor.

Ashley and his men finally reached the Yellowstone River on October 1, 1822. They were greeted with cannon fire and an even more pleasing sight. Major Henry and his men had been busy since their arrival. Fort Henry, a picketed enclosure with log buildings at its corners, stood as a newly built sentry on the Missouri River just above the Yellowstone River. The mood at Fort Henry was good. No other trappers had been seen in the region, and the Henry-Ashley men were well supplied for next season's hunt. The two partners decided that Major Henry would remain and that General Ashley would return to St. Louis to arrange for more supplies and men. Ashley soon boarded a pirogue with a handful of men and the few packs of beaver that had been trapped, and they headed south on the Missouri River.

Major Henry sent out two hunting parties in the fall. One went up the Missouri River, and Major Henry himself led the other up the Yellowstone River. Diah was teamed with a fellow named Chapman and directed to supply Fort Henry with meat and skins, but not to overlook any beaver they could take conveniently. Game was abundant, and they easily accumulated a store of meat for the winter. Their assignment complete, Diah and a few men set out on Major Henry's trail. They met him as he was returning to the fort. An advance party had been left at the Musselshell River, and Diah continued on to their location. They arrived on November 1, just as the ice was beginning to crust the rivers. They took time to hunt, built some lodges and set in to endure the winter. None knew how long or how harsh it would be, but spirits were high.

A winter in the bush was a significant rite of passage for any mountain man. Diah could call himself a *hivernant* (one who has spent a winter in the bush). Evidently, he had also earned the respect of Major Henry, who called on 24-year-old Diah to travel south to meet Ashley's return party with a message that more horses were needed. Henry's scouting had revealed good trapping along the tributaries of the Yellowstone River, but that the territory was difficult to access by water. While the trappers might hike into the region, horses were needed to pack out the beaver pelts. But horses were dear in the Yellowstone country. If Natives could be found who were willing to trade, they demanded double the prices south on the Missouri River.

Diah reached Ashley near the Ree villages on the Missouri in May 1823. Ashley planned to trade with the Natives. The Ree wouldn't have been his first choice—other traders' stories suggested they were fickle and as likely to attack Americans as to deal with them—but Henry's need gave Ashley little choice. On May 30, he anchored his two keelboats midstream and went ashore to open negotiations. The Ree agreed to trade, and Ashley informed them that he wanted 40–50 horses. By sundown on May 31, Ashley had 19 horses, but trading broke off when one of the chiefs demanded guns and ammunition as payment. Ashley sensed trouble brewing, and only the late hour prevented him from leaving. The next day was stormy, and it was impossible for the horses to ford the river as would be necessary to reach Fort Henry. Ashley ordered that a shore command be formed to protect the animals, and he placed Diah in charge.

Diah spent an anxious night on the sandbar below one of the Ree villages and its 600 warriors. Others with him were less worried, and some even ventured into the village for female companionship. All hell broke loose sometime after midnight.

"Stephens' been killed!" cried one of the trappers, as he stumbled onto the sandbar.

"Make sure your powder's dry, boys!" called Diah.

But no Ree appeared until just before daybreak.

"For a horse you can have the body of the white man. But it won't have a head!" taunted a brave.

As night's dark blanket was replaced by morning's pink glow, Ree warriors began firing on the shore party. The trappers were in a terrible position. The Natives were on the slope overlooking the sandbar and were sheltered behind the pickets that surrounded their village. The trappers had nothing but a few cargo boxes and the horses to hide behind, and the horses soon proved of little value because the Ree shot most of them. The thudding of balls and arrows into the splintering boxes was drowned out by the even more harrowing pleading of the men who sought help from those on the keelboats. Diah could hear Ashley barking orders to the boatmen to get the vessels near shore. But the boatmen sensed disaster, and neither prayers nor threats could spur them into action.

"The Injuns are on the beach!" someone shouted.

With that news, the trappers abandoned the fight, made for the river and swam for the boats. Diah was the last to make for the water, firing off a final few rounds as cover for his men. In the river, it was every man for himself. Some of those who had been injured ashore or while swimming sank or were swept away by the strong current. Others swam the 90 feet to the keelboats before the vessels slipped anchor and drifted away. The 15-minute attack by the Ree took 13 lives and wounded 11, which represented nearly a quarter of Ashley's force and didn't include the financial loss of the cargo and horses. The western fur trade had never witnessed such a disaster, and it seemed as if matters were to worsen.

When the keelboats made their escape, the current took them south of the Ree villages. They still had to pass the Natives to get to Fort Henry, and the boatmen refused to continue. A return to St. Louis was out of the question. It would leave the trappers on the Yellowstone River without supplies, and without the pelts from the fall and spring hunts, Ashley would be unable to pay his creditors. The morale of the men fell even more when two of the wounded trappers died. Diah helped to raise spirits when he led the men in an uplifting prayer. Reared at the knees of the Methodist circuit riders back east, he had both the skill and the faith to inspire men.

Diah also had courage, as Ashley discovered when he finally settled on a course of action. Someone would have to travel

overland to Major Henry and return with reinforcements.
Diah, who knew something of the territory, volunteered along
with a French Canadian. As soon as they set out, disappearing
on foot into the woods, Ashley pulled his men back to the
Cheyenne River. He also sent some of the nervous boatmen
south to the military post at Fort Atkinson to inform officials of
the events at the Ree villages. He hoped that the commanding
officer would dispatch a detachment to teach the Ree a lesson.

Diah got through to Major Henry, who gathered the available men and loaded the pelts on pirogues before setting off
down the Missouri River. Assisted by the current and under
cover of darkness, they passed the Ree villages without incident
and joined with Ashley in early July. In late July, Colonel Henry
Leavenworth arrived at the mouth of the Cheyenne River with
five infantry companies (250 troops) of the Sixth Regiment and
hundreds of allied Natives, mostly Sioux, but only about one-
third of them with rifles. Joseph Pilcher and 60 trappers who
worked for Pilcher's Missouri Fur Company accompanied
them. These men were as eager as Ashley to make the Missouri
route safe. Ashley divided his 80 men into two companies and
gave Diah command of one. On August 9, 1823, they attacked
the Ree.

The Ree retreated to their villages under fire. A couple of six-
pounders were trained on the villages, but the assault did not
draw the Natives out. The Sioux tired of waiting, and most of
them left to hunt or forage in the Ree crops. Eventually, a chief
emerged to parley. Leavenworth demanded that the Ree promise better behavior and return Ashley's property. They agreed to
be peaceful but protested that Ashley's dead horses could not
be brought back to life. Leavenworth accepted their promise
and explanation and made treaty. When the Ree delivered only
18 robes, three rifles and a horse, Leavenworth made plans to
attack. During the night, however, the villagers slipped away
undetected. The troops burned the villages in frustration.

The Ree War caused more problems than it solved. Ashley got back little of the $2200 in goods he'd lost to the warriors, and the trappers still had to worry about the Ree, whose anger with the Americans had intensified. General Ashley returned to St. Louis with the pelts to work on financing, while Major Henry went back to the Yellowstone River. They had different plans for Diah, however. Henry gave Diah command of a small expedition of about a dozen men and directed him to explore trapping territory to the west. The goal was to cross the valleys of the Powder and Tongue Rivers on their way to the Bighorn River. They would continue on to cross the continental divide and make the spring hunt on the as-yet untapped west side of the Rocky Mountains.

Diah's expedition, which included Bill Sublette and Tom Fitzpatrick, set off in late September 1823, and it promised to be difficult. The few horses Diah had were used to pack supplies, and so the men had to walk. Fortunately, a few weeks out they were able to trade for additional horses with a band of Sioux. But the new animals tired as they reached the Powder River country later in the fall, and the men were again on foot leading the exhausted animals. Transportation was soon the least of Diah's worries. As the men filed through a narrow valley, Old Ephraim, as trappers called all grizzly bears, lumbered out of the brush. Diah was at the front, and he met the bear head on. Jim Clyman, one of the trappers, described what happened:

> Grissly did not hesitate a moment but sprang on the captain [Diah] taking him by the head first; pitching sprawling on the earth he gave him a grab in the middle fortunately catching by the ball pouch and Butcher Knife which he broke but breaking several of his ribs and cutting his head badly; none of us having any surgical Knowledge what was to be done...I asked the captain what was best; he said one or to

[go] *for water and if you have a needle and thread get it out and sew up my wounds around my head which was bleeding freely…upon examination I* [found] *the bear had taken nearly all his head in his capacious mouth close to his left eye on one side and close to his right ear on the other side and laid the skull bare to near the crown of his head leaving a white streak whare his teeth passed; one of his ears was torn from his head out to the outer rim.*

Clyman followed Diah's instructions as best he could, but Diah was left with only one eyebrow, a torn ear and some jagged scars. He wore his hair long thereafter. Ten days later Diah was riding again. They had not gone far when a party of trappers approached. They were Missouri Fur Company men, sent by Pilcher to keep an eye on the Henry-Ashley men. Competition for the mountain fur trade was heating up.

By February 1824, Diah's party was searching for a pass through the Wind River Mountains. The mountain men had encountered Crow braves a few weeks before, and after Diah's persistent questioning, they had revealed that the streams on the western side of the mountain range were thick with beaver. Diah led his men as far as the summit of Union Pass, but they became snowbound there. Diah decided to return to the Crow, hoping to learn of an alternate route. The Crow suggested they go to the southern extent of the Wind River Mountains, past the Popo Agie and Sweetwater Rivers and cross at the South Pass. The men wasted no time, but travel was difficult in mid-winter, and a few trappers nearly froze to death in the cruel and biting winds. They huddled around the Sweetwater River for some weeks, but by mid-March the men pressed on so as to be in position to carry out a spring hunt.

They cached a few supplies for future use and set out. Within a week, the men made it through the South Pass and across the continental divide to the lands where the waters flowed into the Pacific Ocean. But their arrival in this new land was not as exciting to them as the buffalo that one of the men brought down. Four days of hunger gave a unique perspective to events.

Their presence, however, was a historic event. The men of Diah's party were the first white men to make a westward passage through the South Pass, but more importantly, their accomplishment drew the channel into America's consciousness. The South Pass thereafter served as an important entryway into the lands beyond the mountains.

On March 19, the men reached the Green River. They were excited to find good beaver sign and thought that maybe there was something to what the Crow had said after all. Diah divided the men into two groups and took six south along the river, leaving four others to trap around its head. The two groups met at the cache on the Sweetwater River in June. The melting snows had swollen the river, and Diah built bull boats to ferry the good take of pelts back to Ashley. Diah kept seven of the men with him, and in July, returned west for the fall hunt.

Whether Diah knew it or not, trapping along the Green River placed his men in the southern reaches of territory that the British Hudson's Bay Company (HBC) had been actively trapping for a few years. The British did not have legal title to the region. They disagreed with the United States on a border beyond the Rocky Mountains to the Pacific Ocean and had agreed to share the Pacific Northwest in 1818. Diah was trapping north of the Snake River in September, when he encountered a party of HBC trappers led by Alexander Ross. Ross's party was one of several British outfits working in the region. George Simpson, the energetic and calculating resident governor of the HBC in North America, had ordered his employees to trap out the Snake country so as to make it a fur desert. While the tactic was expected to bring in profits, Simpson also expected that Americans would not push into the territory if no pelts—or economic benefit—could be had. The order was designed to create a buffer between the United States and British territory farther north.

Ross was suspicious of the Americans. He thought that deserters from his own party had guided them into the region, and he was certain that Diah's men were spies intent on interfering with British activities. Diah didn't help the situation. He bristled at Ross's overstated claims that his men were in British territory and insisted that they were on American soil. Nevertheless, Ross allowed Diah and his men to follow his party back to Flathead Post, the HBC advance post on Clarks Fork well to the north. When they arrived there in November, Diah was impressed by the trading relationship maintained by the HBC with the local Natives. It was well organized, friendly and most profitable for the British. Diah did not remain long at the post. Although Ross remained uncertain about the American's intentions, Diah was not held prisoner.

When Peter Skene Ogden left for the Snake country in the summer of 1824 with one of the largest ever HBC trapping parties, Diah and his men joined them. The Americans were pleased to return to familiar territory. Friendly Natives informed him that American trappers were operating nearby, and Diah left the British in mid-April. They were Henry-Ashley men, led by John Weber, whom Diah had last seen in the fall of 1823 along the Wind River.

The Henry-Ashley men traveled south into unknown territory, where a young James Bridger, who was among the party, discovered the Great Salt Lake. They enjoyed good fall and spring hunts, and in July 1825, returned to Henrys Fork on the Green River, the place appointed by Ashley as the site for the summer gathering. Henry-Ashley men, trappers out of Taos, New Mexico (the unofficial southern headquarters of the mountain men), HBC deserters and trappers from other firms joined what would be known thereafter as the rendezvous.

It was to become an important event, one of trading, recreation and storytelling—two weeks of fun to work out the kinks and stresses acquired during 50 demanding weeks in and along western streams. Over the years, the rendezvous became a real whoop-up and the mountain men always greatly anticipated its arrival. They staged competitions, using pelts as gambling chips. Pelts not lost in wagers were used to buy goods brought west by eastern suppliers. Weapons, ammunition and rum were especially popular. So were the trinkets and cloth that smacked too much of civilized life to the mountain men, but which were in great demand by the Native women, who were also important in rendezvous fun.

By nature and upbringing Diah was not inclined to join in many of the rendezvous activities. Folks claimed that he had no vices, and no one ever saw him laughing, so he was hardly popular at the event. Still, he inspired others and did not lack for friendship. And on this occasion, Diah had business matters to consider. At the 1825 rendezvous, it became clear to everyone just how much money was to be made from beaver. Ashley collected nearly 9000 pounds of pelts, worth close to $50,000 in St. Louis. He didn't pay more than $3 per pound to the mountain men, often less, and he also benefited from markups on supplies brought out from the East. Clearly, the businessmen and not the trappers made the real money. So, when Ashley offered Diah the position of field captain, essentially the partnership held by Major Henry who retired in 1824, Diah agreed.

Diah returned to St. Louis with Ashley to collect supplies ordered by the men. In late October 1825, he set off with 70 men, including James Beckwourth, for the Rocky Mountains. After distributing the supplies, Diah disappeared out west. February 1826 found his party at the Great Salt Lake, and Diah set about exploring it, hoping to find a river linking it with the Pacific Ocean. He never found the river, but he developed a fondness

Trappers, Natives and a wagon train gather at the annual rendezvous in Alfred Jacob Miller's *The Cavalcade or Caravan*. Businessman William Ashley introduced the rendezvous to the American fur trade as a creative solution to the problems of provisioning trappers scattered throughout the Rocky Mountains. In 1825, he first directed his trappers to meet on the Green River in the summer to exchange furs for supplies. The rendezvous was an immediate success. To the trappers, who spent most of the year alone or in small camps, rendezvous became popular as a social event, where friendships were renewed and stories were swapped. In a few years, the rendezvous attracted free (independent) trappers and Natives and the gathering took on something of the carnival atmosphere where there was gambling, drinking and womanizing.

for the region, which he soon called his home in the wilderness. He also traveled west to the rim of the Salt Desert. By the summer of 1826, he was back at Cache Valley for the rendezvous. The big news at rendezvous was Ashley's decision to follow Henry's lead and retire from the trapping business. Diah teamed up with Bill Sublette and David Jackson to buy his outfit.

The partners decided that Diah should explore the lands to the southwest to evaluate their trapping value. In late August 1826, the South West Expedition, including Diah and 17 men, set out for the Great Salt Lake. There they turned south and traveled into the heart of northern Mexico. By early October, they reached the Colorado River. Along the way they had encountered and made trading treaties with Ute and Paiute bands. But the journey had been difficult on the men, and when the expedition reached the Mojave Villages on the Colorado River in late October, the situation was dire. They had lost many horses and "had learned what it was to do without food."

The Mojaves were among the most attractive and strong Natives that Diah had ever seen, and they must have been surprised by the rag-tag lot of scrawny white men who showed up so unexpectedly. Nevertheless, the Mojave allowed them to stay and recover.

Among the Mojave were two runaway Natives from the Spanish Mission of San Gabriel in the San Bernadino Valley to the west. Diah persuaded them to guide his party to the mission, which they reached in late November. It was a momentous event. Diah and his men were the first to cross overland from the Missouri River to California. Diah left most of his men at the mission under the most hospitable care of Father José Sànchez and rode south to San Diego, the seat of the governor José Maria de Echeandia. Diah was eager to continue north with his men, a journey that required Echeandia's permission.

But the governor was suspicious of the Americans. He laughed at Diah's claim that his men were hunters. Echeandia thought them spies and suspected that their presence revealed the United States' desire to enlarge its southwestern borders. Eventually, the governor gave Diah a passport, requiring him to take his South West Expedition back on the route by which they'd come.

Diah led his men from the mission on January 18, 1827, but rather than return to the Colorado River, they turned north after leaving the San Bernardino Valley and traveled along the edge of the Mojave Desert. Diah believed that he was outside California and considered his direction legal. He chose the route based on rumors of beaver in the San Joaquin Valley. His men had yet to trap any beaver on the journey, and Diah did not want to return to the rendezvous empty-handed. The rumors of beaver proved true, and by the time the men reached the American River in the spring, they carried 1500 pounds of pelts.

Despite their best efforts, the South West Expedition could not return east to the Cache Valley by way of the American River canyon. Deep snow impeded their progress and made it impossible for the horses to eat. Five of the animals died, and the men were at risk of freezing to death in the cold weather. Diah ordered their retreat to the Appelaminy (Stanislaus) River, where they waited for the weather to turn.

A few weeks later, on May 20, Diah made a second effort to cross Mount St. Joseph, as he called the Sierra Nevada. He chose two men, seven horses and two mules to accompany him. He directed the rest of the men to remain with the horses and pelts and left with a promise to return within four months. Diah's route is a matter of some speculation, but he apparently followed the north fork of the Appelaminy River through Ebbets Pass, and eventually, south of Walker Lake into the Great Basin. It was a significant journey; Diah and his companions

Silas Goebel and Robert Evans were the first white men to cross
the Sierra Nevada, and they lost only two horses and one mule
on the journey.

Throughout June, the men traveled across the Great Basin,
part of which Diah called the Great Sandy Plain. There was no
game and little water to be found in the region, although they
did encounter some Natives who had no clothing and nothing
to subsist on but grass seed and grasshoppers. In late June they
saw the Great Salt Lake, and by the first week of July they were
back at Bear Lake east of the Cache Valley in time for the rendezvous. The small party was greeted by joyous cannon fire from
the four-pounder Sublette had recently brought from St. Louis.

Even without Diah's pelts, Sublette, Jackson and Smith were
able to pay off their debt to Ashley. The future looked good
for the outfit. Once the rendezvous had run its course in mid-
July, Sublette went north to dangerous Blackfoot country, Jackson made for Utah and Diah headed back to California with
18 men to retrieve the trappers and pelts he'd left behind in the
spring.

Diah's men traveled south and learned from a band of Utes
along the Lost River that trappers were pushing north from
Taos. It was competition Diah didn't need. He pushed on to
the Colorado River and the Mojave Villages, where his men
received a much different welcome than enjoyed on his last
visit. The Mojave traded and then, unexpectedly, attacked the
party as they crossed the Colorado River. Four men were killed
when Diah takes up the story:

> *I was yet on the sandbar in sight of My dead companions
> and not far off were some hundreds of Indians who might in
> all probability close in on us and with an Arrow or Club ter-
> minate all my measures for futurity. Such articles as would
> sink I threw to the river and spread the rest out on the sandbar.
> I told the men what kind of Country we had to pass through*

and gave them permission to take such things as they choose from the bar.

They made their selections and moved on in the almost hopeless endeavor to travel over the desert Plain, where there was not the least possibility of finding game for our subsistence. Our provision was all lost in the affray. We had not gone more than half a Mile before the Indians closed around us, apparently watching the proper moment to fall on us. I thought it most prudent to go in to the bank of the river while we had it in our power, and if the Indians allowed us time, select the spot on which we might sell our lives at the dearest rate.

The men constructed a makeshift barricade, tied their knives to stout saplings to make lances and waited.

On one side, the river prevented them from approaching us, but in every other direction the Indians were closing in upon us, and the time seemed fast approaching in which we were to come to the contest which must, in spite of courage, conduct and all that man could do, terminate in our destruction.

It was a fearful time. Eight men but with five guns were awaiting behind a defense made of brush the charge of four or five hundred Indians whose hands were yet stained with the blood of their companions.

Some of the men asked me if I thought we would be able to defend ourselves. I told them I thought we would. But that was not my opinion. I directed that not more than three guns should be fired at a time and those only when the Shot would be certain of killing. Gradually, the enemy was drawing near, but kept themselves covered from our fire.

Seeing a few Indians who ventured out from their covering within long shot I directed two good marksmen to fire they did so, and two Indians fell and another was wounded. Upon this the Indians ran off like frightened sheep and we were released from the apprehension of immediate death.

The Mojave weren't interested in wasting lives to scalp a few mountain men. Following their retreat, Diah scouted the area for a spring he remembered from when he was last there. He found the marker to the south, and the men slipped away in that direction. The remainder of the journey to the San Bernardino Valley was made easier when the party traded for horses with some friendly Ute and Shoshone. In mid-September, Diah found his trappers. He directed them to continue trapping, but took three with him to the Mission San José. Diah sought permission from Spanish authorities to allow his exhausted and injured men to recover in California and travel through it.

Fathers Duran and Viader greeted the Americans with cold shoulders at Mission San José. They were confused by the trappers' sudden arrival and would not listen to Diah when he tried to explain why he was in the country. The priests confiscated the men's horses and demanded that they remain at the mission until a Mexican officer could be brought in from San Francisco to decide if the Americans had any business in the country. Lieutenant Martínez arrived, and he informed Diah that he was to be tried as an intruder into Mexican territory. Martínez sat as unbiased judge and found no evidence of wrongdoing on Diah's part. Diah informed Martínez of his desire to meet with the governor in Monterey. Martínez agreed, and Diah was escorted north. When Diah met with Governor Echeandia, he explained to him that difficult travel conditions had forced him to leave his men behind on his last journey and that he had returned to collect them. The governor was not satisfied with the explanation and suggested to Diah that the whole thing was "a mysterious business." Nevertheless, Echeandia wanted Diah and his men out of Spanish territory, and after negotiations, he agreed to let them sail from Monterey to San Francisco on board the American ship *Franklin*.

Diah sold his beaver pelts, nearly 1600 pounds, to the captain of the *Franklin* for just under $4000. The sale allowed the

Americans to purchase supplies needed for the remainder of their journey. Diah, thinking as a businessman, also purchased 300 horses and mules, which he planned to sell to the trappers at rendezvous. The ship set sail on November 15. A few days later, they arrived at San Francisco and rode for the Mission San José. After collecting his men and writing letters of complaint to Mexican authorities detailing the "Spanish cruelty" that the Americans were subjected to, Diah and his 20-man party rode east on December 30, 1827. The plan was to find and trap the Sacramento River in the spring, move north to the Columbia River, and perhaps continue up the coast to the Russian fort on Bodega Bay. However, the party did little trapping because they had few useable traps left. Diah resigned himself to the fact that 1827–28 would be a year of exploration.

Diah headed north, and his outfit reached the Pacific Ocean north of the Sierra Nevada in early June. The Natives were mostly friendly, but there were occasional skirmishes. Of greater concern to Diah was the harshness of the terrain. During one three-day stretch, 23 animals died. Game was also scarce, and the men often suffered from hunger.

Suffering through one particularly desperate stretch, the party was fortunate enough to encounter a Native band willing to trade for food. The Natives were shrewd bargainers, dividing their supplies into small parcels and demanding goods in return that Diah considered excessive. Still, blubber and a mixture of dried grass and weeds with mussels took the edge off the worst of the hunger pangs.

By late June, they had unknowingly reached Oregon country. Diah suspected that his men were getting closer to British territory because the Natives had trade goods that he recognized as coming from the HBC. Of greater concern was the Natives' interest in the Americans' supplies. At the confluence of the Umpqua and Smith Rivers, a Kelawatset who had been

in the trappers' camp stole an axe. Diah had the man tied up
before he revealed where he'd buried the tool. Unknown to
Diah, the captive was a prominent member of his band, and
once released, he convinced his people of the need for revenge.
Diah was not in the camp when the attack occurred, which was
fortunate for him because three of the four men in the camp
died. The fourth, Arthur Black, fled with a gaping wound to
his back. Black knew that the HBC Fort Vancouver was somewhere to the north on the Pacific Ocean. He headed in that
direction and stumbled into the fort about four weeks later.
When Diah and two companions returned to the camp, the
Kelawatset fired on them. The three also fled north and arrived
at Fort Vancouver, at the mouth of the Columbia River, a day
after Black.

Upon meeting with Dr. John McLoughlin, the chief factor at
Fort Vancouver, Diah insisted that the Kelawatset be punished.
McLoughlin hesitated. He knew that an attack on the Kelawatset would spiral into increased bloodshed and violence, which
would interfere with HBC coastal trade. But McLoughlin was
eager to assist Diah. He knew something of Sublette, Jackson
and Smith and anticipated that Diah might be able to help the
HBC with its problem of deserters. McLoughlin agreed to send
out a party to recover the Americans' lost goods. It was a measured response McLoughlin thought best for business. Diah and
his three men joined the 37-man party when they set out in
early September. Although they discovered that most of the
Americans' supplies were scattered among several bands and
impossible to retrieve, they recovered several horses and mules,
a good portion of their pelts and a collection of other supplies
without incident. The Natives were not inclined to upset their
most important trading partner, the HBC. The men were back
in Fort Vancouver by December.

While at Fort Vancouver, Diah met George Simpson, governor of the HBC who was touring his company's western posts.

Simpson didn't share McLoughlin's concern about the presence of the Americans. His plan to trap out the Snake country and thereby dampen the United States' interest in the region was unfolding nicely, and he didn't hold too high an opinion of the "intruders."

Simpson's snobbish attitude did not endear him to Diah. Simpson did, however, buy Diah's pelts at a reasonable price and allowed his men to winter at the fort. The layover gave Diah time for reflection, and he grew worried about British strength in the region. He feared that strong British relations with the Natives, combined with a British naval presence on the coast might well make it impossible for the United Stares to control, and ultimately possess, the Pacific Northwest.

Diah prepared to return east with Simpson in the spring of 1829, but when he learned that American trappers were in the south near Flathead Post, he decided to go there instead. To his surprise, his partner David Jackson was there. Jackson had good news: the company had paid off the season's debt without Diah's returns. After a successful fall hunt, Diah wintered on the Wind River. He took time to write to his family. A letter to his brother Ralph suggests that life in the West and the events since his departure in 1822 weighed heavily on him:

> I have passed through the Country from St. Louis, Missouri, to the North Paciffick Ocean, in different ways—through country's of barrenness & seldom one of the reverse, many Hostile Tribes of Indians inhabit this Space, and we are under the necessity of keeping a constant wach; notwithstanding our vigilence we some times suffer; in Augt. 1827 ten men, who were in company with me, lost their lives, by the Amuchabas [Mojave] Indians, on the Colorado River; & in July 1828, fifteen men who were in Company with me lost their lives, by the Umpquah [Kelawatset] Indians....As it respects my Spiritual welfare, I hardly durst speak. I find

myself one of the most ungrateful, unthankful Creatures imaginable. Oh when shall I be under the care of a Christian Church? I have need of your Prayers....may he, before whom not a sparrow falls, without notice, bring us, in his own good time, Together again.

Diah took a party, including James Bridger, into the Powder River country for the 1830 spring hunt. They knew that there was plenty of beaver in the region, but they were not easily taken because the Blackfoot, who lived in the area, doggedly resisted white intrusion. The Blackfoot harrassed Diah's men constantly, and in one major blow, stole 30 horses and 300 traps during a raid along the Bighorn River. Diah decided to pull his men out of the territory. By July he was back at the Wind River for the rendezvous, where change was in the air. Diah met with his partners to discuss the future of the trade. They agreed that increased competition and a falling beaver population were sure to cut into profits. Diah was also eager to return East. His mother had died recently, and he longed to be with his family. Sublette, Jackson and Smith sold their operation to the Rocky Mountain Fur Company. Diah eventually cleared over $20,000 for his interest in the outfit and the furs from the last hunt.

Diah completed his business dealings, said his goodbyes and headed for St. Louis in early August 1830. He arrived there a few months later and tried to settle down. He bought a house in St. Louis and used his wealth to help family and a few childhood friends. But Diah soon hankered again for western trails. He had money to invest, and in early 1831, partnered with old trapping friends Bill Sublette and Tom Fitzpatrick for a trading venture to Santa Fe. With 80 men and 22 wagons, they made for the Santa Fe Trail in April.

The territory was new, and the journey was challenging. Gros Ventre and Pawnee warriors harassed the men. When they crossed the Arkansas River and entered the scorching Cimarron Desert, the need for water became a problem. Diah set out with Fitzpatrick in search of a spring. Sometime after the pair separated, Diah stumbled upon a Comanche hunting party of 15–20 warriors. Flight was impossible, so Diah placed all hope in putting up a courageous front and rode up to the braves. They surrounded him. A crack split the dry desert air, and a ball struck him in the back. With the last of his energy, Diah shot and killed the Comanche chief before the warriors attacked him. Jedidiah Smith died May 27, 1831, at the age of 32.

CHAPTER SEVEN

Christopher "Kit" Carson
1810–1868

CHRISTOPHER "KIT" CARSON was only a year old in 1811 when his family pulled up stakes in Madison County, Kentucky, and moved to Howard County, Missouri. His Scottish father, Lindsay, possessed a pioneering spirit, longing to know what lay over the next horizon. Those first years in Missouri were fearful ones lived under constant threat of Native attack during the War of 1812. Kit spent his earliest years inside a crude fort—the settlers' log cabins close together and barricaded. Sentries were also posted at the ends of the fields to protect the farmers. Otherwise life went on much as in any pioneering community. Kit's family grew, and his mother, Rebecca, would eventually give birth to nine more children.

Kit's father had dreams that his son might get an education and perhaps become a lawyer, but those dreams died with him when a falling tree took his life in 1818. A few years later his mother remarried, and Kit was apprenticed to a saddler in nearby Franklin. The town, on the Missouri River, was the most western settlement in the territory. From it snaked the trails that led to the Rocky Mountains and points beyond—Oregon,

California and Mexico. Kit hated saddlery, but he loved listening to the men who had traveled those trails, many of whom visited his master's shop for equipment repairs. Their stories made Kit itch to see the places and to live the adventures these bushy-bearded and buckskin-clad men described.

Kit kept his ears open for news of western-bound trading parties. In late 1826, he found one to his liking, much to the displeasure of his master. On October 6, a notice appeared in the *Missouri Intelligencer*.

> *To whom it may concern: That Christopher Carson, a boy about 16 years old, small of his age, but thickset, light hair, ran away from the subscriber, living in Franklin, Howard County, MO, to whom he had been bound to learn the saddler's trade, on or about the first day of September last. He is supposed to have made his way to the upper part of the state. All persons are notified not to harbor, support, or subsist said boy under penalty of law. One cent reward will be given to any person who will bring back the said boy.*

When the notice appeared, Kit was already pleading his case to Charles Bent, one of the owners of the prominent western trading operation, Bent, St. Vrain and Company. Bent was preparing his mule trains for a trip to Santa Fe. He chuckled at the sight of the small pup and his grand dreams of striking west, but Bent himself had started in the business around the same age. He sensed that the boy had spunk.

"All right, Kit. In the morning you'll go with the train. You'll herd the cavvy," declared Bent.

Kit grinned widely. He had only his father's old flintlock rifle, a blanket and a tin cup given to him by Bent, and he had no idea what the cavvy was, but he was going west!

Kit discovered that herding the cavvy—the spare animals— along the often-dry trails and penning them up at each stop was hard, thirsty work. But he proved himself, and it wasn't long before he was taking his turn guarding the wagon train for four hours every third night. Sleeping under the stars had a certain romantic appeal, even if his bed was the hard ground. But the night was always cold and occasionally wet, so Kit congratulated himself when he spotted an old, abandoned Native lodge and sneaked inside for cover. Perhaps he wondered why no one joined him. He soon learned a hard lesson when he woke up covered with lice. Kit spent painful days tormented by the graybacks until a kind soul suggested that he throw his clothes on an anthill. The ants devoured the lice, and after he shook the ants out successfully, Kit finally stopped scratching.

Kit reached Santa Fe in November. Not liking the town, he collected his pay in Mexican silver and joined a party of mountain men headed for San Fernandez de Taos, New Mexico, the southern meeting place of the mountain men. It wasn't much of a town, home to about 500 when busy, however, Kit was attracted to its strange mixture of whitewashed adobe houses, reddish Native pueblo dwellings and simple, stripped-down trapper establishments. Kit spent the winter in Taos, listening to the mountain men whose old bodies could no longer withstand the pain of trapping in icy creeks. By the time he left to search for work in the spring of 1827, he had learned to speak Spanish.

Kit found jobs hard to come by, but he bounced around for a few years working as a hand on caravans that took him across the Cimarron Desert and along the old Santa Fe Trail. He worked as an interpreter in Chihuahua, a teamster in the Gila River copper mines and as a cook in Taos, but he couldn't find a steady job, and by 1829, he was ready to return to Franklin. With some regret, he decided to sell his father's old hickory stock flintlock rifle to raise money for the trip. He thought Ewing Young, a Taos trader who ran his own trapping outfit, might be interested in buying it. He found Young at his house, which was decorated with mounted animal heads, thick pelts and full of leather-tough mountain men.

"Mr. Young, I got this here rifle to sell. Might ye be buying?"

Young took a look at the young man, still hardly more than a boy. He had seen Kit around town and knew something of his story.

"I kin always use a good rifle, boy," replied Young, as he balanced the rifle in his hands. "I can especially use it now as I'm readying a brigade to trap into Mexico. You interested?"

"In trappin'?" gasped Kit.

"I'm not talkin' about dancin', boy," chuckled Young, to the laughter of the men.

"Yes sir," blurted Kit, who thought of Franklin no longer.

It was illegal for Americans to trap in Mexico, so Young led his 40-man brigade north, but only far enough to convince prying eyes that his intent was to trap in the United States. Fifty miles out, the party swung south and made for the Rio Gila, where Kit discovered that Young had more than trapping on his mind. The year before, Apache warriors had attacked one of Young's brigades, and he wanted revenge.

Young got it when the brigade encountered the Natives who had attacked his people at the head of the Salido (Salt) River. Kit wasn't at all sure that he'd made the best decision to sign on with Young when he heard the scouts describe the approaching river banks as covered with Apache. But the good humor of the trappers, who were anxious for a scrap, and his employer's cool demeanor and quick thinking eased his nerves. Young ordered most of his men to conceal themselves, anticipating that a camp with few men would be attractive to the Apache. His reasoning was sound; it wasn't long before the braves advanced on the camp. When they were near the fires, Young barked the order to shoot.

Kit, who had been hiding under a blanket, threw his covering off, rose on surprisingly steady legs with the stock of his flintlock wedged against his shoulder and fired at the nearest Apache. Kit saw the blood spread across the brave's chest before he collapsed. Kit's heart was thumping; he had taken his first coup—trapper lingo for killing a Native. Later, he hammered a brass tack into the flintlock's hickory stock as the trappers did to tally their coups.

After the Apache were routed, he found it difficult to suppress a smile when he overheard Young observe, "Kit's a likely youngster. He'll make a mountain man yet."

Kit certainly felt like one, but there was plenty more to do and learn before he could lay claim to that lofty title. He earned more of Young's respect a few months later, when the brigade was in California. While trapping on the Sacramento River, the padre who operated the Mission San Rafael approached Young. Some Native converts had fled from the mission and taken refuge with a band hostile to the missionaries. The padre wanted Young to get them back. Young agreed and selected Kit to lead a small party of 11 trappers and a few Spaniards. Kit found the band's village and demanded the surrender of the fugitives. When the band leaders refused, Kit attacked. The Natives retreated, and Kit ordered their village burned. Against a backdrop of smoldering lodges, he asked again for the fugitives. They were turned over without hesitation.

Successful in his first command, Kit enjoyed a triumphant return to San Rafael.

Young began to think of the teenager as his right-hand man, and he increased Kit's responsibilities. He led a few other retaliatory raids against Natives who had crossed the brigade, but Kit didn't remain with Young much longer. By early 1831, he was back in Taos with several hundred dollars that he'd earned as his share in Young's trapping and trading enterprise.

"We passed the time gloriously," said Kit, "spending our money freely, never thinking that our lives had been risked in gaining it. Our only idea was to get rid of the dross as soon as possible, but at the same time have as much pleasure and enjoyment as the country could afford."

Kit found particular enjoyment in the liquor known as Taos Lightning and in gaily-dressed senoritas. But recreation was expensive, and by summer's end, Kit was broke. It was around that time that Tom Fitzgerald of the Rocky Mountain Fur Company arrived in town looking for recruits. Kit was as anxious to get back to the simpler life of a trapper as he was to make money, so he signed up. The party headed north to the Sweetwater River and trapped until the creeks froze over. Kit enjoyed a good fall hunt, taking enough beaver pelts to cover his outfitting debt to Fitzgerald plus 200 pounds of pelts. They wintered at the head of the Salmon River, and Kit could finally claim that he was a *hivernant* (winterer), a true mountain man.

Kit met James Bridger that winter and had to suffer through the worst of the trapper's tall tales. While other mountain men chuckled at Jim's stories of giants and their elephant ponies who lived on an island in the Great Salt Lake, Kit wasn't about to discount the stories and made a mental note to steer clear of the place. In April they broke winter camp, and Kit linked up with Captain Gaunt, an acquaintance from Taos, and he spent the rest of the year traveling and trapping around the South Platte and Arkansas rivers. But Kit didn't approve of Gaunt's trading practices with the Natives. He used sweetened alcohol—a mixture of pepper, tobacco and tallow—to take advantage of them. Kit liked his booze and didn't care too much for the Natives, but he was a principled man and drew the line at dishonest practices.

In 1832, Kit signed up again with Bent, St. Vrain and Company. Early the following year, a band of Crow warriors stole some of the trappers' horses while they were camped on Wild Horse Creek. Because the animals were hard to come by and therefore expensive, their loss was a substantial one, so the trappers planned to recover them. Kit hadn't lost a horse, but he joined the party willingly, declaring, "there is always brotherly affection existing among trappers, and the side of danger is always their choice." A dozen trappers and two Cheyenne visitors set out in search of the Crow.

Kit and his companions traveled most of the next day through deep snow, and at nightfall, they spotted the fires of the Crow camp in the distance. They tied their exhausted horses to trees and made a slow advance on the camp. Anxious to avoid detection, they crawled the better part of four miles, until they were close enough to see what they were up against. The Crow were divided into two camps and, by their behavior, it was clear that they weren't expecting to be pursued.

"Look at those bastards!" exclaimed one of the trappers. "They got a right fandango going to celebrate the raid."

Kit could only grunt his agreement as he watched the Crow sing, dance and make merry.

"There," Kit whispered. "Near the camp to the east. That's where our horses are tied up. There's no way we can take 'em now. Must be at least 50 braves in the camps. Best wait till they bed down."

No one could disagree with Kit's reasoning, so they spent damp, cold hours lying in the snow until the camp fell silent. Then the party split. Six men carefully made their way to the horses, while the other six remained in position to offer support in case of trouble. Kit was among those sent to retrieve the horses. He was suddenly thankful for the snow he'd cursed all evening because it allowed them to approach the camp without making any sound. They circled around behind the horses, threw snowballs at the animals and drove them back towards the other six men. The raid went far easier than any had expected, and once they were far enough from the camp to avoid detection by any of the Natives, they discussed what should be done next.

"We got our horses, so let's head back to camp," suggested one of the men.

"I agree. No sense in pushing our luck," added another.

But three trappers, including Kit, were not yet willing to return.

"We had no horses to recover, yet we endured a day of hard travel and a night of bitter cold to help you fellows. We want satisfaction," declared Kit.

The others pointed out that the consequences of an attack on such a large Native party could be serious, even fatal.

"Well, damn the consequences," barked Kit. "Ain't never stopped us before."

After much haranguing, the others finally agreed to join them.

"We might be fools," suggested one of the men, "but we won't miss out on the fun!"

The trappers tied the recovered horses up with their own and retraced their steps to the Crow camps. They were just ready to attack, when a dog caught their scent and barked wildly. The men could hear the Crow shouting at the alarm, but before the braves could prepare a defense, the trappers opened fire. Many Crow were killed in the onslaught, although some escaped into the woods where they remained hidden until the morning. In the light, the Crow discovered the small size of the party that had attacked them. Angrily, they launched a counterattack. But Kit and the trappers remained calm and killed five more Crow. The braves regrouped for another assault. They were finally successful and forced the trappers to retreat. But the Crow were in no mood to press their advantage, and they returned to their camps. The trappers hurried back to their horses.

"During our pursuit of the lost animals we suffered considerably," admitted Kit, "but in the success of recovering our horses and sending many a redskin to his long forgotten home, our sufferings were soon forgotten."

A few months later, Kit was at Bent's Fort (near present-day La Junta). Also there was the band of the two Cheyenne who had been with him during the attack on the Crow. They told the story to their chief, Yellow Wolf, who was impressed by Kit's bravery.

"My son, I give you a new name. You have won it," declared Yellow Wolf. "From where the sun now stands, your name is Vihhiunis, Little Chief."

Kit returned to Taos in October 1833 with plenty of pelts and a desire to forget about mountain life for a time. The locals made forgetting easy. They always prepared a fandango for the returning mountain men, a celebration where the hard-won profits of trapping were transformed into bottomless barrels of booze and where friendly senoritas danced tirelessly. Kit lived hard for a few weeks and loved every minute of it. But by month's end, he was ready to get back to the mountains, so when Captain Stephen Lee, a partner of Bent, St. Vrain and Company, came calling, Kit signed up. Lee's party headed north on the Spanish Trail, eventually holing up at Robidoux's trading post on the Windy River in Ute territory when the snow began to fall.

In March, after wintering at Robidoux's, Lee's party met up with Tom Fitzpatrick and James Bridger on the Snake River. Lee sold his goods to Fitzpatrick and returned to Taos, while Kit remained on the Snake. He took a few men with him and moved to the head of the Laramie River to trap. Kit then moved on to the Green River for the annual trapper rendezvous, the closest thing to a Taos fandango that could be found north of the Rio Grande. It was also an opportunity for mountain men to trade pelts and to restock supplies.

In September 1834, Kit set out with a party of 50 men to trap before the fall freeze up. It was a wretched hunt. The trappers

Kit Carson in the mid-1860s, after fighting with the Union in the Civil War. He resigned his commission as a general.

were in Blackfoot territory and were constantly being harassed by warriors, who succeeded in killing five men. Finally abandoning the futile exercise, the trappers returned to their winter camp on the Snake River. But the Blackfoot had not forgotten them. In February, warriors raided the trapper camp and stole 18 horses. Kit and 12 others set off in pursuit.

The heavy snow delayed the Blackfoot, and the trappers caught up with them after a few days. The trappers called for a parley, and the Natives agreed. But it soon became clear that the Blackfoot weren't interested in talking.

A mountain man named Markhead marched out to meet one of the warriors halfway between the two parties. He returned looking skeptical.

"Chief says they figured we was Snake Injuns. Don't want no trouble with the whites."

This brought a few guffaws from the men. Blackfoot thinking they were Snake. Hah! But the Blackfoot had them outnumbered better than two to one, so the trappers thought it best to continue the parley. The two parties agreed to lay down their arms and smoke together. When the Blackfoot brought out five broken-down horses to return to the trappers, the men went for their weapons. Kit and Markhead were at the front, and they chased two warriors into the trees. Kit was trying to get a good line on one of the fleeing Natives when he noticed that the other had Markhead in his sights. Kit changed targets and brought down the warrior with one shot. Then he saw the rifle of the other Native pointing at him. Without enough time to reload, he dove for the bushes. He heard the crack of the rifle before he landed, and he felt the ball graze his neck and strike his shoulder. The trappers withdrew, and Kit endured a painful night that was made all the worse because they were afraid to light a fire that might show the Blackfoot their position. They returned to the scene of the fight the next day and discovered that the Blackfoot were still there. The trappers decided that they should retreat to their winter camp and return their attention to trapping.

Perhaps it was the injury and the temporary loss of independence that set Kit to thinking about finding a woman. Plenty of mountain men had Native companions, and by most accounts, the arrangement was highly beneficial. Kit remembered the advice of trapper named Blackfoot Smith, with whom he'd lived a few years back at the Robidoux post.

"What a mountain man wants is an Injun woman—one who can pack a mule, make meat, dress robes, make moccasins, cook, pitch a lodge, ride all day and then give birth to a likely youngster after sundown. When I come home at night, froze stiff with cold and starvin', I can see the big yaller lodge all lit up like a lantern among the pines, and I know when I go in, there the old gal will be, with a good fire burning and the kettle steamin'."

Kit thought he could use a little tending, and he set his mind to taking Smith's advice to "trap a squaw."

He set his sights on a pretty young Arapaho, Waanibe, who he met at the Green River rendezvous in 1835. But Waanibe had also attracted the attentions of a strapping Frenchman named Shunar. He was strong, intimidating and mean and, as Kit put it, "made a practice of whipping every man that he was displeased with—and that was nearly all." Kit didn't like the man, and their shared interest in Waanibe meant the sentiment was mutual.

Waanibe chose Kit, which thoroughly humiliated Shunar. He got drunk and tried to take Waanibe by force. When that failed, Shunar turned his anger on the first trappers he could find. Kit, who had heard of his attack on Waanibe, came looking for Shunar. He saw the unconscious and bloody bodies of his friends, who had been unfortunate enough to have fallen within Shunar's sights, and steeled his jaw.

Shunar, his blood still hot, declared, "I can take Frenchman, Spaniard, Injun. And if an American wants some of me, I'll cut a switch from the nearest tree and whip him."

Kit had endured Shunar's overbearing and violent ways long enough and he replied, "I'm the worst American in this camp. And if you keep talking like that, I'll rip your guts."

Shunar made for his gear and reappeared mounted, with rifle in hand. Kit grabbed a pistol, leapt onto his own horse and galloped up to the Frenchman.

"You planning on shooting me?" demanded Kit.

"No," replied Shunar, even as he raised his rifle.

The two weapons cracked together with one sound. Shunar jerked on his horse, as the ball passed through his arm. The powder from Shunar's shot burned Kit's eyes, but the ball only trimmed his long hair and grazed his neck. He wore the scar for the rest of his life. Shunar was quiet for the rest of the summer.

Kit married Waanibe, who he called Alice, before heading out on the fall hunt. And although he didn't talk much about her in polite company in later years, he thought highly of her, once revealing, "She was a good wife to me. I never came in from hunting that she did not have the warm water ready for my feet."

Kit spent the next few years trapping along the Yellowstone and Missouri Rivers and their tributaries. The money in trapping was good with a prime pelt bringing in $6, and in the mid-1830s, plenty of beaver could still be found. During this time, Kit led his own party, known throughout the region as the Carson Men. Kit's reputation as a truthful and reliable man who knew where the beaver were ensured that he had no trouble attracting trappers to follow him. By the close of the 1830s, however, the heady trapping days of only a few years previous were gone. Trappers were more plentiful, and most of the traditional hunting regions were trapped out. During the rendezvous of 1839, Kit teamed up with James Bridger and headed for Blackfoot country. The journey was dangerous because the Blackfoot were among the fiercest Natives on the Plains, and their dislike of whites had long discouraged mountain men from trapping in their territory. But the expedition had the potential to make considerable profit, and in strapped circumstances, that was enough for the trappers.

Kit led an advance party, and when they reached the Missouri River, they encountered a small party of trappers. Some were wounded, the result of a recent run-in with the Blackfoot.

Thinking the Blackfoot long gone, Kit decided to wait for Bridger's party, and in the meantime, set a few traps. Most of the men had done so and returned to the camp, when two trappers exploded through the trees, out of breath.

"Blackfoot," one gasped, "fired on us. Big band, a ways back and they're makin' for here."

The trappers jumped into action, building a temporary fort of stone and trees into which they also herded the animals. The Blackfoot arrived a few weeks later with more than 1000 warriors (to Kit's 60 men), but they were not inclined to attack the fort for fear of losing too many men. Instead, the two parties exchanged gunfire and arrows throughout the day, but try as they might, the Blackfoot could not drive the trappers out. They didn't give up.

Kit smelled something. He saw the column of smoke and shouted, "Fire!"

The Blackfoot were trying to burn them out. Kit gave them credit for a good strategy, and as he watched the flames creep closer along the grass towards the trees, he heard some of the men talk about making a run for it. Unexpectedly, when the fire was close enough for the trappers to feel the heat, it died out.

"I cannot account for our miraculous escape from the flames," admitted Kit, "unless it was the protecting hand of Providence. It could scarcely have been anything else, for the brush where we were concealed was dry and as easily burned as that which had been consumed."

Kit may have thought it Providence, but the superstitious trappers were calling it "Kit Carson's luck." Before the day was out, Bridger arrived with the rest of the brigade, and the Blackfoot retreated. The Natives continued to harass the trappers until they left the region a few weeks later.

Although he maintained his own band of mountain men throughout the 1840s, Kit found the returns of trapping increasingly poor. A trapper was fortunate to take sufficient pelts to pay for his traps, so most began looking for other work. Charles Bent, Kit's old friend, hired him as a hunter to supply Fort Bent. Traders also paid Kit to ride the Santa Fe Trail and some of the lesser-known routes along the Arkansas River to keep out the whiskey traders, who were causing trouble with the Natives. He spent time in Taos, and in early 1842, Kit returned to Franklin. Alice, his wife, had passed away, and he wanted to ensure an education for his daughter Adeline in civilized country.

Kit quickly tired of the settlements, as he called them, and boarded a steamer bound for the upper Missouri River. Also on board the steamer was Lieutenant John C. Fremont, who was under orders from the chief of the Bureau of Topographical Engineers to survey the Platte River and the South Pass in the Rocky Mountains—the route taken by Oregon-bound immigrants. Fremont was looking for a guide, and Kit volunteered his services. The lieutenant made some inquiries, liked what he heard and hired Kit at $100 a month, a most attractive salary.

Kit came to like and respect the man. When they reached Fort Laramie, they were warned that the Sioux were on the warpath and likely to attack.

Fremont replied, "I have been sent by the government to perform a certain duty, and no matter what obstacles lay before me, I will continue my march and accomplish my mission or die in the attempt. If my party is slain," he added confidently, "the government will punish its destroyers."

It was a statement of duty that Kit understood. The Sioux never did attack, but Fremont's party endured troubles nonetheless. The men stayed in army tents, and Kit considered them to be an example of the worst use of canvas. He eventually took his concerns to Fremont and advised the lieutenant to purchase a Native tipi. After Kit assured him of the comforts and value of such a lodge, the open-minded Fremont bought one from some local Natives. He ordered Kit to pitch it, but

John C. Frémont (1813–90). When Lieutenant John Frémont hired Kit Carson in 1842 to guide his survey team through the South Pass of the Rocky Mountains, the 39-year-old lieutenant had already participated in one successful expedition for the United States Corps of Topographical Engineers. On completing his fifth and final expedition in the mid-1850s, Frémont had explored thousands of miles of territory between the Missouri River and Pacific Ocean. His maps and publications popularized and, ultimately, opened the West to settlers. Frémont fought in California in the Mexican War and later for the Union in the Civil War. In 1856 he ran as the Republican nominee for the American presidency. Twenty years later he served briefly as territorial governor of Arizona.

unfortunately, no one knew how to put it up because that was woman's work. Throughout the afternoon they argued, cursed and struggled with the poles and the hide coverings. Late in the day, they finally had something standing but it hardly resembled a tipi, eliciting great guffaws from those who saw it. Eventually, the Native wife of one of the men went to work on the tipi and had it standing in 15 minutes. Then she spent the next few days training Fremont's men on how to do the job.

Kit left Fremont in September after the surveying was complete. Fremont's subsequent report emphasized Kit's value on the mission, and the mountain man's reputation began to spread in the East, even though Kit knew nothing of it. By late 1842, he was back in Taos. A young senorita had caught his eye the last time he had been in the town, and Kit had been unable to stop thinking about her. In early 1843, 33-year-old Kit married 14-year-old Josefa Jaramillo, the daughter of a prominent New Mexican family. Kit remained with her for a few months before signing on as a hunter with a northern-bound Bent, St. Vrain and Company wagon train. Upon reaching Fort Bent, he caught up with Fremont, who was embarking on a second expedition to Oregon and north California. Kit offered his services, and Fremont was glad to have him on board.

The party explored the Great Salt Lake, the western reaches and mouth of the Columbia River and the Great Basin, eventually crossing the Sierra Nevada into the Sacramento Valley. They visited John Sutter's impressive rancho, not yet made famous by the discovery of gold. In April 1844, Fremont's outfit headed home, making a risky crossing of the snow-choked Sierra Nevada to the south and joining up with the Old Spanish Trail. Along the Mojave River, they ran into a Mexican man and boy who had a story to tell.

"My name is Andreas Fuentes," said the man. "The boy is Pablo. We were a party of six—my wife, Pablo's parents and a friend—out of Pueblo de los Angeles [present-day Los Angeles].

Josefa Jaramillo, the Taos beauty who Kit married in 1843, and their child

Several Indians met us. They seemed friendly and left us alone. We were happy. A few days later, 100 Indians attacked our camp. They shouted and fired arrows at us. We had 30 good horses, and they wanted them. Pablo and I ran the horses off and left them by a stream to search for help. I don't know what happened to the rest of our party," concluded a sobbing Fuentes.

Fremont directed his party to the place where Fuentes had left the herd. They found no horses.

"Will someone help me get them back," pleaded Fuentes.

"Volunteer if you wish, men. I'll even give you horses to ride," said Fremont.

Kit and a man named Godey agreed to join Fuentes. Fremont gave the Mexican an encouraging slap on the back.

"You'll find those horses, Fuentes," assured Fremont. "You've got one of the best trackers on the Plains helping you," he added, nodding to Carson.

The trio wasted no time setting out, but Fuentes had to turn back after 20 miles because his horse gave out. The next day, Kit and Godey spotted the Native camp, which they guessed held about 30 braves. They hobbled their own horses and crawled in among the herd, hoping to run them off before the Natives noticed. But one of the animals snorted, alarming the rest.

As the braves rushed for their weapons, Kit and Godey quickly decided to charge the camp. Kit killed a brave with his first shot, and Godey brought one down with his second. The Natives fled after the unexpected attack, likely assuming that many more men were invading their camp.

Godey tossed Kit his rifle and unsheathed his knife to scalp the two braves. They then rounded up the horses and headed back to the place where the Natives had attacked the Mexicans. They found the mutilated bodies of the two men and later the bodies of the two women in grisly states. Fuentes, however, reclaimed his herd.

Fremont was impressed and wrote as much in his official report: American newspapers picked up on Fremont's report, and wide-eyed easterners were soon reading about a courageous, selfless mountain man, but Kit was unaware of his soaring reputation. In July 1844, he left Fremont at Bent's Fort and headed back to his wife in Taos. Indeed, just as he was becoming well known, 34-year-old Kit decided to settle on a farm on the Cimarron River, some 55 miles east of Taos. Perhaps he took a look at the 19 brass tacks in his rifle's stock and figured it was best not to press his luck.

But Kit's life as a farmer was short-lived. He was still clearing land for his spread when Fremont sent word in August 1845. He was embarking on another expedition, this one around the Great Salt Lake and into California, and wanted Kit as a guide. Kit had promised Fremont that he would join any future explorations, so he sold his spread for half its value and made for Bent's Fort.

"That was like Carson," said Fremont, "self-sacrificing, prompt and true."

The party explored the headwaters of the Arkansas River and then headed west to the Great Salt Lake. Fremont revealed that he wanted to cross the Great Salt Desert, but Kit was none too enthusiastic because he had heard old trappers speak of the impossibility of the task. There was neither water to drink nor grass for the animals. But the challenge was not insurmountable, as proven by Jedidiah Smith who had crossed it in 1827. Fremont was no less determined than Smith, and he was a persuasive leader. The party made the crossing without incident.

Exploring California proved more difficult. They encountered a small party of hostile Natives and killed all of them. More disturbing was an order from General Castro, the Mexican commander in California, who was suspicious of Fremont's mission, especially given that the United States and Mexico were on the verge of war. He demanded that Fremont leave California or risk being attacked. Fremont objected to the high-handed treatment and refused to retreat. Instead, he made camp, surrounded it with hastily built fortifications and set an American flag above it. The two sides exchanged gunfire, but Castro did not attack. Fremont soon tired of waiting and decided to set out for the Columbia River.

While Fremont's party was near Klamath Lake, at the southern end of the Cascade Range, two tired and worn men stumbled into the camp. They were members of a party led by Lieutenant Gillespie of the United States Marines. War had erupted with Mexico, and American officials in California ordered Gillespie and a small command of six others to find Fremont and have him return to California. But Gillespie's horses had given out, and he was forced to make camp. Fremont chose 10 men, Kit among them, and headed for Gillespie's camp. They reached it after nightfall. Gillespie had important dispatches for Fremont, and while he read them, Kit cleaned his rifle, breaking it in the process. He still had his pistol, but as Kit pulled his saddle blanket over himself for the night, he felt mighty uncomfortable.

Kit hadn't yet drifted off to sleep when he heard an unexpected thud. He looked across the fire and called to the man lying there.

"Basil, that you?

But there was no reply because Basil Lajenesse was dead, with a tomahawk buried in his skull.

Suddenly, Kit saw the Natives in the shadows.

"Injuns in the camp!" he hollered, as he jumped up.

They were Klamath and known to be hostile. Everyone was up quickly, but there was confusion. Kit watched as one of Delaware in his own party grabbed a rifle to fend off the approaching warriors. The rifle wouldn't fire, and the man fell with five arrows in his chest.

Kit pulled out his pistol and charged the Native with the biggest war bonnet. He assumed it was the chief and thought that his death might chase off the other warriors. The ball from his pistol only knocked the tomahawk from the warrior's hand. Kit fell back and watched as the chief took two more balls before he collapsed. Kit thought him the bravest Native he had ever seen and was relieved to see him dead.

On returning to the main camp at Klamath Lake, Fremont informed the men that they were heading back to California. He sent Kit ahead with 10 men to ensure the route was clear of Natives. The party made it back to California by May 1846, and they joined in the Mexican War. Kit continued to serve with Fremont.

The fighting took an odd turn for Kit in July. Word reached Fremont that General Castro was in Los Angeles preparing for a new offensive. Fremont, still in the Sacramento Valley, decided that he could best catch Castro if he sailed from Monterey to San Diego. He arranged for the sloop *Cyane* to transport his men. When they boarded the vessel, Commodore Stockton, commander of American forces in California, enlisted them as the Navy Battalion of Mounted Riflemen!

A seasick Kit cursed every minute of the 400-mile voyage and told anyone who would listen that if he could get back to the mountains, he'd fight every Native he saw single-handedly rather than go back to sea. Thankfully, his tour as a seaman was short-lived. When the *Cyane* arrived at San Diego, Castro had already fled. The riflemen took possession of Los Angeles in August, and a month later, Fremont sent Kit to deliver dispatches to Washington describing the victory in California. It was an honor, and Fremont meant the assignment to reward Kit for his service. Kit took 15 men, and they made it as far as the Rio Grande. They encountered General Stephen Kearny and the Army of the West en route to California where they thought a battle with the Mexicans awaited. Kearny ordered Kit to join his outfit as a guide, and before year's end, Kit was back in California.

The Army of the West discovered plenty of fight left in the locals, but Kit worried that the rash Kearny was not the best man to lead the American forces. His concerns were justified. At San Pasqual, 50 miles from San Diego, Mexicans ambushed the Americans, killing 36 soldiers and officers, and injuring others, including Kearny. Kearny burned with revenge and wanted to push his men after the Mexicans, despite their exhaustion, hunger and thirst. His officers, with Kit's help, persuaded him to remain camped until reinforcements arrived. All that was needed was someone to sneak out of camp and get word to Commodore Stockton in San Diego. The assignment was perilous because Mexican soldiers remained nearby, but Kit volunteered along with Naval Lieutenant Edward Beale and a young Native.

"As soon as it was dark, we started on our mission," said Kit. "To avoid making noise while crawling over the rocks and brush, we took off our shoes and fastened them under our belts. We could see three rows of sentinels, all mounted, and we would frequently have to pass within 20 yards of one. We finally got through, but we had to crawl about two miles, and having the misfortune to lose our shoes, we had to travel barefooted over a country covered with prickly pear and rocks. We reached San Diego the next night, and Commodore Stockton immediately ordered 160 or 170 men to march to General Kearny's relief."

When the Mexicans saw the approaching army, they fled. Kearny joined up with Stockton in San Diego, and they marched on Los Angeles, which was no longer under American control. With the support of six cannon, the Americans had little difficulty winning the battles of San Gabriel on January 8, 1847, and Los Angeles on the following day. Kit, who had been laid up for some time after the daring relief mission to San Diego, didn't do much fighting in those battles. Fremont arrived soon after the victory, and Kit remained with him throughout much of the winter.

In late February, Fremont ordered Kit to Washington to deliver dispatches to the War Department. There he met with President James Polk, who was most interested in Kit's observations on California. Polk appointed him Lieutenant of Rifles in the United States Army and asked Kit to return to California with dispatches for Kearny and Stockton. With a 50-man escort to ensure the journey was successful, Kit arrived in October. There he was assigned to Captain Andrew Smith of the First Dragoon Regiment.

Kit spent the winter fighting Native raiders, and in May 1848, set out for Washington with another saddlebag full of dispatches. Along the way, Kit considered abandoning the mission. While in Santa Fe, Kit learned that the United States Senate had refused to confirm his commission as a lieutenant. Rumors had it that Kearny was behind the opposition. No rank and no pay for the last two years of work! Kit's friends advised him to wash his hands of the dispatches. But Kit was a man of his word, unlike those eastern politicians.

"I considered the matter, reaching the conclusion that as I had been chosen as the most competent person to take the dispatches through safely, I would fulfill the duty; if the service I was performing was beneficial to the public, it did not matter to me whether I was enjoying the rank of lieutenant or only the credit of being an experienced mountaineer. I had gained both honor and credit by performing every duty entrusted to my charge, and on no account did I wish to forfeit the good opinion of a majority of my countrymen merely because the Senate of the United States had not deemed it proper to confirm my appointment to an office I had never sought."

Kit fulfilled his obligation and returned to his wife in Taos in October 1848. It was the first time he had been able to put his feet up in months, and he found that he enjoyed it. At 37, he figured he was getting too old to continue making a livelihood as he had. He decided to end his roving ways in order to make a home for his family. He partnered up with Lucien Maxwell, and they built a ranch at the Rayado Valley, 50 miles east of Taos. They had put in a hard summer's work when, in October, a party of soldiers and civilians arrived from Taos.

Apache had attacked an immigrant train and had taken a woman named Mrs. White and her child as prisoners.

Kit signed up as a guide. The Apache, experts at leaving confusing tracks, tested his skills, but Kit finally led the party to their camp. Kit prepared to attack, but the commanding officer, Major William Grier, ordered him to stand down so that Grier could parley with the Apache chief. As Grier approached the camp, the Apache shot him. Fortunately, the force of the ball was spent when it struck him, and he wasn't injured seriously. Grier ordered a charge, but it came too late to save Mrs. White, whose warm body they found after the Apache fled.

Kit thought her death was for the best because "the treatment she had received from the Apache was so brutal and horrible that she could not possibly have lived very long. Her friends should never regret her death. She is surely more happy in heaven, with her God, than among her friends on this earth."

Kit and the others continued their pursuit of the Apache, eventually attacking their camp and killing one warrior. Kit had a most sobering experience as the men searched the Apache belongings. They found a book called *Kit Carson, the Happy Warrior*, in which he was portrayed as a great hero who had slain hundreds of Natives. It was the first revelation of his eastern popularity. But he couldn't enjoy it.

"I have often thought," he confessed, "that Mrs. White must have read it, and knowing that I lived nearby, must have prayed for my appearance in order that she might be saved. I did come, but I lacked the power to persuade those that were in command over me to follow my plan for her rescue."

Kit spent a few years ranching in Rayado, occasionally assisting authorities in apprehending criminals or tracking Natives who raided his herds. He also worked as a guard for immigrants on the Santa Fe Trail, which was much plied by outlaws since the Mexican War. He drove mules to Fort Laramie and guided a wagon train to St. Louis. On his return from St. Louis, he dropped in at Bent's Fort. There weren't many acquaintances to renew. Trade was slow, and William Bent was the only old timer he recognized. In the spring of 1852, Kit organized one last trapping expedition up to the South Platte and Arkansas Rivers. He rounded up 18 of his old buddies and made a good hunt, but when he returned to Rayado, Kit knew it would be the last ride of the Carson men.

Still, Kit found it difficult to stay in one place for long. He drove sheep to California and took some time to visit San Francisco. He was amazed by the changes brought by the gold rush of 1849. He reached Rayado on Christmas Day 1853, and discovered that he had been appointed Indian agent, a position which he held throughout the late 1850s. The local Natives respected Kit.

William Sherman, who would become general of the army, revealed something of the mountain man's standing among them: "These Red Skins think Kit twice as big a man as me. Why, his integrity is simply perfect. They know it, and they would believe him and trust him any day before me."

Kit's duties were a mixture of administration and fieldwork. For an illiterate man, Kit's bureaucratic responsibilities were challenging. He visited different bands to expound on the value of peace, and he greeted Natives at his office in Taos. He guided several expeditions against the Apache, and he also managed to arrange a council with the Ute to the north. Unfortunately, the Ute fell victim to smallpox around the time of the council and blamed the Americans for it. They joined the Apache in waging war. Kit was pleased when the governor called for volunteers to fight the Natives.

When the Civil War erupted in 1860, Kit's sympathies lay with the Union. He had fought Natives and Mexicans for the good of the United States, and he didn't want to see his nation torn apart. Kit volunteered and was appointed lieutenant

Kit Carson, dressed in finery that would have elicited playful barbs from his mountain men friends

colonel of the First New Mexican Volunteer Infantry. His regiment first saw action in the Battle of Valverde on February 21, 1862, and it was likely the only time he fought Confederate soldiers. Soon after he was detailed to fight Natives, who were taking advantage of the white man's war by stepping up their raiding. Throughout 1862–64, he led successful campaigns against the Apache and Navajo. But Kit met his match in the Comanche and their allies.

In November 1864, Kit, who was a colonel by this time, marched his 400 men (including 75 Natives) down the Canadian River to Adobe Walls, an abandoned fur-trading post in the Texas Panhandle. He planned to use the location as a base from which to bring the raiding Comanche into line. As they approached Adobe Walls, scouts informed Kit that many Natives were in the region. Kit figured they'd soon meet in battle because he'd had a dream that revealed a big fight, and he was a superstitious man who believed in such things. He was right. On November 26, his men arrived at Adobe Walls to find the Kiowa camped there. Kit's troops sent the Kiowa fleeing, but the Natives soon returned with their Comanche allies, over 1000 warriors. For a time, the troops had an advantage because of their two howitzers, but the warriors pressed and fought with uncommon bravery. Kit was forced to retreat. It was a decisive defeat, and Kit never denied that the Natives licked them at the Battle of Adobe Walls.

After the Civil War, Kit saw no more of the adventures that had spiced his life. He resigned his commission—he was a general—in 1867 and returned to Josefa. She died shortly after in childbirth. Kit moved to Fort Lyon where he could be closer to a doctor. At 58, the demands he had made on his body were finally taking their toll. In the spring of 1868, he asked the cook to fix him up a meal of buffalo steak. The doctor told him it would likely do him in. Kit ate it anyway. He asked for his old clay pipe. When the bowl of tobacco was spent, he started to cough and brought up blood. Kit died on May 23, 1868, and was buried next to Josefa at Taos.

CHAPTER EIGHT

John George "Kootenai" Brown
1839–1916

DARK DAYS BLANKETED IRELAND when John George Brown was born in County Clare in 1839. Potatoes rotted in the ground, threw a foul stench over the countryside and brought starvation to the land. The famine or the disease that accompanied the rot took John's parents when he was young, and his grandmother Bridget Finucane raised the boy. While money was tight, Bridget managed to ensure John's education, but it proved more difficult to provide him with a future in a country that was in disarray. Bridget looked to the military, where members of John's family had previously found employment and honors. Many letters to military authorities all brought the same reply: John might have a commission, if he purchased it. Life in service of his country seemed out of reach.

The military's attitude changed dramatically in 1857 when Britain was in sudden need of soldiers to fight in the Great Indian Mutiny on the Asian subcontinent. On December 13 of that year, John was commissioned as an ensign without purchase and assigned to the Eighth Regiment. After spending the first months of 1858 training in England, Brown was given command of a 21-man unit that endured a long ocean voyage aboard the *Octavio* and arrived in Calcutta in February 1859. They were quickly marched to Fattehguhr in north-central India, only to discover that the rebels had been brought under control. Those young soldiers who had talked of adventure and hatched schemes for glory soon discovered that the real challenges would be bowel discomfort and fever tremors. With little to do, the men began watching and participating in the local culture. John found himself drawn to eastern mysticism, which would flower into a lifelong interest.

The Eighth Regiment was recalled in December 1859, and John left India in April. Frustrated with the confining rules and regulations that governed life in the army, John decided to resign his commission. It was difficult to break the news to his grandmother, who had done so much to assure his military career. And when he finalized his resignation in September 1861, John had no desire to muck about in Irish mud for the rest of his life. Military life had given him a taste for adventure, and he hungered for more. In the closing days of 1861, he joined his friend Arthur Vowell and boarded a steamship for Britain's Pacific colony of British Columbia, where gold had been discovered in 1858.

The journey took the men across the Isthmus of Panama to San Francisco, a city that had grown as a result of its own gold rush in 1849. That rush had since played itself out, but not before transforming San Francisco into a major economic center. This was good news for Brown and Vowell, who needed money to continue their journey. They were soon employed as skinners, driving a horse team hauling furs from the city's old docks to its business district. It was difficult, unpleasant work given their inexperience with horses. The old dockside was a collection of jutting piles, sharp angles and rotting timber planks, so it took considerable skill to maneuver a team while ensuring that none of the horses tripped or plunged

through a hole and broke a leg. Only the liberal use of pro-
fanities and a judicious application of the whip brought any
success. With a short-fused temper that found ready expression
in words and actions, John had few problems.

In February, Brown and Vowell boarded the *Brother Jonathon*
for the short journey north to Victoria. That dot of civilization
was, by the decree of Governor James Douglas, the required
point of departure in the colony for anyone who wanted to trek
into mainland British Columbia and prospect for gold. Victoria was no San Francisco. While it had a substantial population, it retained much of the character of its first English
immigrants—fur traders and employees of the Hudson's Bay
Company—including a partiality for law and order. Douglas
was also comfortable with those qualities and demanded that
the rule of law extend into the diggings. When Brown and Vowell made their way inland after a brief stint in Victoria chop-
ping timber to replenish their poke, they headed for a place
where prospectors could dig without fear for life or possessions.

The journey up the Fraser River was difficult. The river's rage
combined with a growing awareness that no claims would be
left to stake along it dampened the pair's spirits. Vowell
returned to Victoria, but Brown remained determined to swing
a pick. He took a job with one of the many transportation
companies that shipped goods upriver. The pay was good,
partly because traders could charge outrageous prices for goods
inland claiming freight costs as the reason. But the work was
backbreaking. Powerful downstream currents required the men
to go ashore and haul the 30-foot canoes upriver with long
ropes. When the river was too turbulent or shallow, the goods
had to be packed on the men's backs, often over rough terrain.
At least John and his fellow crew members could relax on the
return journey. The same distance going upstream that took
four and a half days could be covered in two and a half hours
going downstream!

With winter came a shutdown in transportation operations, and John spent the cold months wandering north along the Cariboo Road. Gold had been discovered farther inland, and rumors abounded that claims were still available. Before he got to the diggings, however, he partnered up with a few fellows to trap marten. It proved a good decision because he pocketed $3000 for three months work. Then, in the spring of 1863, he was hired as a constable for Wild Horse Creek, a mining town in southeast British Columbia. With news of a recent gold strike, the town buzzed with activity, not all of it legal.

Constable Brown was chewing on his generous moustache while relaxing near Galbraith's Ferry on the Kootenay River, when the ferry's owner approached him with bad news.

"Constable, I'm afraid we've been duped," said Galbraith, as he handed Brown a small, bulging pouch. "Fool's gold."

John sized up the pouch, tossing it gently in one hand.

"Feels about right," he decided.

Then, he untied the knot that enclosed the pouch and poured the contents onto his hand.

"Looks real good, too," he observed. "Nice nuggets."

"It's high quality, Brown," agreed Galbraith. "That's the reason I took it, no questions asked. Later, when I got a chance to test it, I discovered it was mostly copper, with a little gold and lead. A fine and crafty amalgam. I don't know how they gave it the realistic shape, though."

"I remember a case up on the Boston Bar," replied John. "Seems some counterfeiters had taken to tossing molten metal from a height to bang it up a bit and give it the shape of real nuggets. Could be the same method. Recall the folks who passed it?"

John got a description, made some inquires and discovered that the three counterfeiters were squatting in a one-room cabin on the outskirts of town. He made his way there and knocked on the door. No answer. John slipped his Colt .45

from its holster and threw open the door. In the dusky interior he saw one of the men move for a rifle resting against the far wall.

"That'll be the last move you ever make, partner," Brown snarled. "Reach for that ceiling, or your carcass'll be a lead mine."

Quickly calculating the odds, the outlaw decided they weren't in his favor. He surrendered, but while John tied him up, the other two fled. John was angry. One out of three was a poor average, so once his captive was behind bars, John formed a posse to hunt down the others. The pursuit was short-lived. On the first night, the posse spotted the fugitives' fire, surrounded the camp and arrested the pair without incident. While they were skilled counterfeiters, they were poor frontiersmen, not realizing that men on the run best enjoy their meals cold.

Eventually, John had a stake sizeable enough to allow him to make a run at prospecting. He partnered up with four others and bought a claim near the mouth of Wild Horse Creek. Mostly, John panned for gold, but he also took his turn operating the sluice box, a long two-sided wooden trough that allowed for more efficient prospecting. But even efficiency couldn't discover gold where none was buried, and the men decided to sell the claim. They got $500 and a horse for it. The money was easily divided among the men, but the horse was another matter. They settled on poker, and the game ended with John holding all the chips.

The partners hadn't yet given up on their dream of striking it rich, so they gave some hard thought to where they should stake their next claim. Thinking that the Fraser River and the Cariboo were played out, they decided to head for Fort Edmonton on the North Saskatchewan River, where they'd heard rumors of strikes yet to be made. Unfortunately, all the men knew of Fort Edmonton was that it lay east of the Rocky Mountains.

Heading that way in the autumn of 1865, they slipped through the South Kootenay Pass and were greeted with a sublime vision of nature—crystal lakes, sloping hills and soaring mountains—that touched Brown deeply.

"Boys, I have seen glories such as this only in my dreams," he declared. "This is the place for me."

But not yet. There was still the matter of Fort Edmonton and gold. And as seductive as that dream was, it was forgotten when the men crossed the last of the rolling foothills. Before them lay the great prairies and a massive herd of buffalo that seemed to stretch before them to all points on the compass. The men shot an animal, and for the first meal of many to come, John feasted on buffalo. As they wiped the grease from chins and beards, they considered a new problem. How could they continue on in the face of such a great obstacle? Fortunately, they discovered that the buffalo were docile, and when the men approached, the great herd simply parted, allowing them to continue on their journey.

A long simmering argument about the location of Fort Edmonton boiled over at Seven Persons' Creek (near present-day Medicine Hat). John wanted to follow the foothills north, but the others decided to keep moving east. Of course, John didn't know anymore about Fort Edmonton than did his companions, but he'd heard bone-chilling stories of the hostile Blackfoot. The men were traveling in Blackfoot territory, a foolish route by John's estimation, and it almost cost him his life. As they were camped one night, Blackfoot arrows exploded out of the night. Brown took one in his side, and only the creative and painful use of turpentine, generously poured into the wound, saved his life.

As he recovered, John cursed the men for his injury, and it's a wonder they didn't up and leave him. John had a talent for creative blasphemy, and when his temper was roused, the air became blue around him. Finally, he declared that he'd had enough. Let the others go where they wanted in search of gold; he had almost lost his life and was ready to move on. Back at Wild Horse Creek, he had heard stories of Fort Garry (present-day Winnipeg), somewhere to the east, and he decided to head for it. He set off along the South Saskatchewan River.

After weeks of travel, John stumbled into the community of Duck Lake. It was still a good distance from Fort Garry, but most of the Métis he encountered were from that eastern settlement. They had traveled west, as they did each year, in search of the buffalo on which they depended. As winter was about to set in, John took them up on their offer to remain. He formed an attachment to the free-spirited and devout people whose ancestry was both Native and white, spending the winter learning their ways and their French-Cree patois. When spring arrived, he continued his journey to Fort Garry, reaching it six weeks later.

John set himself up as a trader in Portage la Prairie, about 60 miles from Fort Garry, serving small bands of friendly Cree and Chipewyan. Usually, the trade went smoothly with John exchanging clothing, sugar and booze, among other things, for furs. The locals frowned on trading booze to the Natives because they feared its effects. But it was difficult to avoid because the Natives often demanded a kettle of firewater before they'd even unpack their furs. Nevertheless, John learned about the potent mix of Natives and booze when he was helping out at Johnnie Gibbons' trading post. Some Santee Sioux, refugees from Minnesota, had come in to deal. Trading opened with the customary booze offering, but eventually, John cut them off. Later in the day, the angry Santee attacked the post and killed one of the traders. Everyone else expected the same fate. Fortunately, they were able to get word to a nearby settler, who arrived with 20 others. The Santee fled, but John learned his lesson and thereafter exercised greater caution when trading with Natives.

Tintype of Kootenai Brown, age 28. He wore the distinctive moustache for the rest of his life.

It would be some time, however, before John put that lesson to work. Soon after the violence at Portage la Prairie, he returned to Fort Garry, where he heard that an American businessman was looking for express riders to carry army mail between Fort Abercrombie, Dakota and Fort Benton, Montana. Brown headed south and joined Charles Ruffee's operation. He was stationed at Fort Totten, and his route required him to ride into the dangerous region around the Knife River, where Black-foot and Sioux came to hunt and trade. The Americans considered the two tribes to be the most hostile and aggressive on the midwestern Plains. The Natives, in turn, held a particular disdain for American soldiers, and they saw express riders as soldiers without uniforms. Those the Sioux captured were often tortured and sometimes killed.

John learned of the Natives' hatred and the reasons for it when the Sioux captured him on one of his runs. He listened as Chief Marhpisskat spoke.

"Not many moons ago, the prairies were black with buffalo. But wherever white men go, the buffalo disappear. The death of the buffalo means the death of the Sioux. Look at you in your warm, new clothes," spat Marhpisskat. "You are the friend of the buffalo killers, and they provide for you. Look at me. I am a chief, dressed in rags. For me, their enemy, there is no warmth and comfort."

Luckily for John, someone in the war party knew that he was not an American. Marhpisskat let him go with a stern warning, "Know that he who rides for the soldiers is no different from a soldier. Should you be taken again, you will die."

John hurried away, glancing back to see the smoke rising from the dispatches that had been set ablaze. But he soon forgot Marhpisskat's warning. When Ruffee's outfit went out of business in early 1868, John signed on with the U.S. army to deliver mail between Fort Totten and Fort Stevenson. In May, he had good reason to reflect on his memory failure. Brown left Fort Stevenson with a Métis named Joe Martin, and before they could deliver their dispatches, Sitting Bull captured them.

Sitting Bull had not yet emerged as a great Sioux leader, but he was already known and feared by many on the Plains. Sitting Bull ordered the carriers stripped and their breeches dropped to a chanting chorus of "Kash-ga! Kash-ga!"

Both men could speak Sioux, and they knew that the braves wanted to kill them. But Sitting Bull was not so anxious.

"There is no hurry," he declared. "Prepare a fire, and then the fun can begin."

Sitting Bull was less inclined to give explanations than was Marhpisskat, but the pair knew that whatever death he had in mind would not be quick. They had to act fast. Martin told Sitting Bull that they were both Métis. It was a long shot, but perhaps Sitting Bull would not kill fellow Natives who were not enemies. Sitting Bull could see that Martin was Métis, but he had his doubts about John. However, in the twilight, his long dark hair, deeply tanned skin and his command of the Sioux language gave Sitting Bull pause for thought. The carriers were left alone as the warriors discussed their fate.

"I'm not sure what their plans for us might be, Joe," muttered John, "but I think we'd best make a break for it."

"If we do, they'll shoot us," replied Martin. "But hell, that beats being burned alive."

The two men rolled into a nearby coulee and slipped into a lake. When the Sioux discovered they were missing, the pair was already hiding in the thick bulrushes near the shore. The Sioux shot wildly, but didn't hit their mark. A day later, Brown and Martin stumbled into Fort Stevenson, naked, muddied and bloodied. After a full report to the fort's commander and a good meal, John slept until well into the next day.

John had finally learned his lesson. He quit carrying the mail but stayed on with the army as a civilian employee, operating a store, guiding the occasional party and, when money was tight, carrying a dispatch or two. In the fall of 1869, his duties took him to Pembina, a mostly Métis community near the Canada–U.S. border, where he met and married Olive Lyonnais. "Olivia" and John returned to Fort Stevenson, where they remained until the summer of 1874, when John found his services were no longer needed.

John, Olivia and their young daughter returned to her people and remained with them for three years. The Métis welcomed Olivia's husband as one of their own, and John felt at home with a people who met life on terms similar to his own Irish folk. They enjoyed a story and a song and felt that both were improved when the liquor flowed. But they worked hard when it was required, and never were they more industrious than when hunting buffalo. The Métis economy depended on the great shaggy beast, and John's community followed the herds across the vast territory bounded by the Saskatchewan and Milk Rivers.

John loved running the buffalo as much as any Métis. To the uninitiated, the hunt appeared chaotic. A troop of Métis approached the herd, and at a word from the captain, an experienced hunter chosen by the men, exploded into it. Thundering hooves, bellowing animals, cracking muskets and shouting men were all obscured behind clouds of thick, brown dust. Until the animals scattered and the dust settled, no one was sure how many animals had been killed or if any Métis had been thrown from their runners and trampled. Usually, the animal count was high because a man's reputation rested on his ability, and few were ever hurt because their skills were well honed.

On one occasion, however, John was thrown from his horse and suffered the pounding of frenzied hooves. While he escaped with only a broken shoulder blade, his recovery took some time. As he sat in his tent one Sunday morning, avoiding the weekly Catholic service, he heard a distant rumble that soon caused his lodge to tremble. He knew the sound. A herd of buffalo was stampeding towards the camp!

John grabbed his rifle and leaped from the tent, his pain masked by adrenaline and his resolve. The herd was almost upon the camp, and it showed no intention of veering off. John realized that the efforts of one man would be futile, but he fired a couple of shots that had all the effect of an irritating black fly.

John stood awestruck by the buffalo herd's raw power. It upset tents, reducing many to tatters, and overturned carts as if they were toys, destroying wheels and shafts in the process. And like a prairie thunderstorm, the stampede was over almost as soon as it had begun. All that remained of the herd's presence was a path of destruction through the camp's center. Had the Métis not been praying, the human toll would have been staggering.

Eventually, John itched to move on, and in late 1876, he joined a group of wolf hunters, men hired by ranchers to cull the ferocious animals that ravaged their herds. The following spring, John traveled to Fort Benton, Montana, a major supply center on the northern Missouri River, to sell the hides. He got more than he bargained for. In the heat of an argument, John killed a French trader named Louis Ell and was put on trial for murder. John pleaded self-defense, but a witness testified to his aggressive rage during the attack. And the local sheriff, John J. Healy, claimed he was an unredeemable character. John wasn't at all confident during the trial, and in desperation, he tried to take his own life. When that failed, he resigned himself to the jury's decision. Fortunately, the jurors knew that on the frontier a man sometimes had to provide his own justice, and they acquitted Brown. He later told a friend that "not guilty" were the two most wonderful words in the English language.

John gathered up his family and headed north. He didn't stop until he reached Kootenay Lakes, the place he had seen when he first broke through the South Kootenay Pass more than a decade earlier. He teamed up with Fred Kanouse, a businessman operating out of nearby Fort Macleod, and in late 1877, opened a trading post at Kanouse's cabin on Upper Kootenay Lake. He traded mostly with the Flathead and the Kootenay and enjoyed long hours competing with them in games of chance and skill. John soon sold out his interest to Kanouse and built his own cabin farther along the lakeshore. He did a little trading, but mostly hunted and fished, often selling the game and fish in Fort Macleod. Reports in the local paper trumpeted his abilities and his knowledge of the region, and soon he was called Kootenai Brown. His services as a guide were in great demand. Over the years Kootenai's clients included many adventure-seeking ordinary folks as well as powerful politicians, notably the Minister of Customs and future Prime Minister Mackenzie Bowell, and the occasional English aristocrat.

In September 1883, Brown was contracted by the owners of the nearby Oxley Ranch Company to guide them on a hunting and fishing trip into the Kootenay Lakes area. Two of the owners were the Earl of Lathom and A.S. Neil, who was a member of the British Parliament. They were somewhat surprised when they reached Kootenai's cabin and found a wild-looking, longhaired man in a slouch hat, strange leather garments and moccasins, a man for whom any European heritage appeared but a distant memory. However, Kootenai's reputation preceded him, and the party did not let appearances derail their adventure. Kootenai took them fishing on Lower Kootenay Lake and then south towards Goat Mountain for some hunting. Neither the fishing nor the hunting was good, but the party's disappointment was tempered with stories from Brown's great repertoire of adventures.

They were camped in the shadow of Goat Mountain, enjoying some of his lordship's brandy, when Kootenai began a sad tale.

"Boys," he said, as he pointed to the east, "the Blackfoot call that range the Shining Mountains, and they can be as beautiful as the name suggests. But nature can also be fearful in these parts, and when it is, that shine can mask awful terror.

"The highest peak in the range is the Sofa Mountain. A few years back, a Kootenay Injun was hunting near there. He had better luck than us. At least it started out that way when he found fresh sign of a couple of mountain sheep. He followed them about halfway up the mountain before he finally shot them. Now, it's the practice of the Injuns that the men hunt, and the women dress," Kootenai explained, "so he returned to camp, and the next day he went back up with two women. While they were busy skinning and cutting up the sheep, the brave found more tracks. He left the women and continued on up the east side of the mountain. While he was gone, a freak snowstorm hit, wrapping the mountain in white. The temperature fell like a stone."

"With no warning?" asked Lathom.

"In the mountains, the weather can change faster than the time it takes to load and fire a Hawkens," answered Kootenai. "The next day I was asked to lead a search party. I knew there was little hope, but I agreed. My party found the two women dead, embraced under the bloody and ragged sheepskins for warmth. We continued on and soon found the brave, also dead. In front of him was a pathetic collection of twigs and boughs that he'd tried to use as kindling for a fire. The few matches he'd had with him were burnt and scattered on the ground. Rather than suffer through the cold, he tried to shoot himself with his rifle."

Kootenai paused for a moment, as he recalled the grisly sight.

"A rifle's not suited for that kind of work, and you could tell by looking at him that he'd made a messy job of it. For all his efforts, the cold got him, just like it did the women. We brought him back to where the women were and built a stone cairn around all three."

Kootenai took a swallow of brandy.

"Yup," he concluded, "there's great pleasure in these mountains, but there's great sorrow, too. *Ecce signum.*"

Lathom raised his eyebrows in surprise at the mountain man's use of Latin.

" 'Look at the proof,' indeed," the earl translated. "I, for one, will never again look at these mountains in quite the same way." The others expressed a similar sentiment.

Despite the dangers of life in the mountains, Kootenai loved living there. He had an affinity with nature and never felt quite as content as when he was riding along a sloping crest or a winding river. For the most part he preferred solitude, so that he might contemplate life's bigger mysteries, but he also enjoyed visiting friends at the nearby North-West Mounted Police post or the massive Cochrane Ranch, where he shared many a keg of whiskey. He was often away from his cabin. On one such occasion in the spring of 1885, he returned to find that his wife had died, and that the hired man had buried her body and tended to the needs of the three children. Kootenai felt terribly guilty, so he turned to booze to ease his pain, but not until after he had addressed the matter of his children. Olivia wanted them educated, and Brown was eager to fulfill her wish because he knew that he was not up to the challenge of raising youngsters. He gave them into the care of Father Lacombe, a well-respected local missionary, and it was the last he ever saw of them.

Kootenai was still depressed when Jack Street, a local Mountie, dropped by a few weeks later to check up on him. The two had been good friends for some time and had spent many days hunting and prospecting in the mountains, or just enjoying the scenery. As Street approached the cabin, he heard his friend long before he saw him. Kootenai was deep into one of his rants, using language strong enough to peel the bark from trees. As a Mountie, Street had encountered the lowest of the low, so foul language was hardly unfamiliar to him, but Kootenai's artful expressions made even Street feel like blushing. The Mountie reached the edge of the clearing, where he saw Kootenai taking a stick to a black bear. Not as big as its grizzly relative, the bear was still one of nature's more imposing forces. Kootenai placed every bit of strength from his wiry body into the whupping, pausing only to catch his breath.

"A good workout, eh, Kootenai?" called Street.

"Damn bear," Kootenai replied, when he spotted Street. "I was low on firewood, and wanted to haul some from down by lake's end. The bear's been gone for days, and I had to do it myself."

Street realized that this bear was the one that Brown had raised from a cub and trained as a pack animal. Brown threw the stick down at the feet of the cowering animal and walked to the cabin. Street led his horse over to the hitching post, and tied him up. As he left it, the horse snorted skittishly. Street looked around to determine the problem. There, at the opposite edge of the clearing, was another bear.

"Looks like we got some more company, Kootenai," said Street, as he pulled his rifle from the sheath attached to his saddle and indicated the bear with a tilt of his head.

Kootenai looked over to where his friend had signaled. He motioned to Street to lower his rifle. After a moment's silence and consideration, Kootenai called the name of his pet bear.

"Healy?"

Slowly, and submissively, the bear trotted over. Both men looked over to the discarded stick and saw the wild bear scamper off into the woods. Brown simply shook his head, while Street had a good laugh.

"I'll put on the kettle," Brown said, finally. "What's news from town?"

"It hardly beats the story I'll have to tell to folks," chuckled Street. "Kootenai Brown, fearless mountain man, taking on wild bears with nothing more than a strong piece of willow."

They entered the cabin, and as they sat at a roughly hewn homemade table, Street told him of the recent uprising of Métis and Natives led by Louis Riel in the Saskatchewan valley. Many were worried because Riel had led another successful rebellion 15 years earlier in Red River. While the Saskatchewan valley was far from Fort Macleod, Street informed Brown that a militia, the Rocky Mountain Rangers, was being organized

Rocky Mountain Rangers, formed in response to the North-West Rebellion, at Medicine Hat in 1885. Kootenai Brown, chief scout, is on the far right.

to ensure that the violence didn't spread. Kootenai thought of his days with the army. He didn't care to be ordered around anymore, but he figured that volunteering might help him forget recent painful events. He rode back into town with Street and did just that.

When Kootenai was signed up as a chief scout, officers and troops alike smiled. His knowledge of the land was unsurpassed, and his experiences certainly qualified him for his duties. Everyone felt a little more confident with Kootenai at the head of the outfit. It was a confidence that wasn't really needed because the Rocky Mountain Rangers saw little action. But Kootenai didn't complain. As he confided to a friend, he was more interested in drinking Jamaica Ginger and having a good time than he was in chasing bad guys. He got more than his share of laughs watching the undisciplined company drill, and he had a captive audience to listen to his stories by evening campfires, which were usually the highlight of the day's activities.

Warmed by cups from a bottomless pot of coffee, the men sat around a popping fire, its sparks dancing into the dusky night, smoking rolled cigarettes and pipes or chewing tobacco and listening to Kootenai.

In the spring of '65, me and my pals cashed in our gold mining claims along the Wild Horse Creek in the Cariboo, and set out for Fort Edmonton. First time I saw the Kootenay Lakes. As we emerged from the foothills onto the plains, we all knew we were entering into Blackfoot country, and we didn't know what to expect. Remember, back in those days there were only a few white men—missionaries like Father Lacombe—until you reached Edmonton. The towns that dot southern Alberta weren't even dreams then! It's not like the Blackfoot knew much about our kind, and we knew little about them, save for their warlike ways.

He finished off his coffee and called for some whiskey. His whistle wet, he continued on.

We stopped near Seven Person's Creek and bedded down for the night near a clump of cottonwoods. Our bedrolls weren't even warm before a shower of arrows rained down on us. We had met our first Blackfoot war party. The five of us dove for cover among the trees, and brother, let me tell you that every last one of us thought that we'd reached the end.

Kootenai shuddered at the memory.

There were 30 young bucks in all, and they were out for bear. They rode bareback and used a rawhide halter that went through the horse's mouth. They didn't have any guns, but I can assure you they made the most of those arrows. They soon flushed us out of the trees, and we made for the ridge of a coulee, where there was some low-lying brush. As we ran, we fired our rifles wildly at anything that moved. It was slow going, though, as we were using old muzzle-loaders with balls and caps. Our mouths were full of ammo. It was more luck than skill that brought down two of their party.

Soon, they tired of the game and moved on, stripping buck-naked and swimming across the Saskatchewan, but not before one of their arrows found its mark in my side, just above my kidney. I feared that was it for me. I'm not much on God, but I prayed for His forgiveness as I clutched the arrow's shaft with two hands and gave it a sharp tug. My flesh burned as the obsidian point ripped through the small hole. It was over two inches long, it turned out—I still have it. It might as well have been two feet long. In those days we had no medicine, so we had to use our imagination when dealing with injury. I brought out a bottle of turpentine and got one of my pals to do the doctoring. I bent over, while he popped the cork and inserted the neck of the bottle into the wound. I think he poured about half a pint of the vile stuff into my body, and I don't know that the pain caused by that wasn't worse than that of the arrow itself. It must have been good medicine, though, because within a few days, the pain had gone, the wound had healed up, and the injury never again bothered me.

The next day Kootenai took some of the men down near the river where they had camped. They found two Native skulls and dug five balls from the cottonwoods. Kootenai hadn't told them the night before, but they were camped at the very spot where his adventure had unfolded.

For his tour of duty, Kootenai received a grant of 320 acres from the government. He took the land in the Kootenay region and slipped back into his comfortable Rocky Mountain lifestyle. Hunting, fishing and guiding were punctuated by long evenings spent by the fire reading a volume of Shakespeare or Plato from his considerable library. While folks sometimes referred to him as a mountain man, Kootenai was more learned than most so labeled, with his lifelong love for learning and his penchant for deep and considered reflection on intellectual matters. Many would have been surprised to know that his visits to town took him to the local debating club as often as to a watering hole or the race track.

Kootenai soon tired of living alone. The solitude was bearable, but the chores were never ending. Around 1886, a Cree trading party arrived to do business, and Kootenai made an offer for one their women. They settled on five ponies, and Kootenai had his second wife, Chee-pay-tha-qua-ka-soon (Blue Flash of Lightning). While she didn't share Kootenai's interest in erudite matters, her skill around the campfire and with hides proved to be an asset. Soon, Chee-pay-tha-gua-ka-soon, whom Kootenai called Isabella, accompanied him on his guided trips.

Throughout the 1890s, Kootenai was involved in many of the activities that defined the history of the Canadian West. The Canadian Pacific Railway hired him to pack goods during its construction years. The North-West Mounted Police contracted him to break horses. He dabbled in the illegal liquor trade and got as much joy out of eluding the authorities as he did from drinking the booze. He was one of the first to exploit the Kootenay region's oil resources. Kootenai knew about oil deposits from local Natives, who'd long used the thick, black liquid for medicinal purposes. Kootenai began sopping it up

Kootenai Brown and his wife Isabella, taken between 1910 and 1916, towards the end of Brown's career as a civil servant at Waterton Park

with blankets, packing it in barrels and selling it to ranchers who then spread it on their cattle to protect them from the merciless black flies.

In the late 1890s, the dangers of a life in the mountains were again brought home to Kootenai. On one cold winter day, as he sat in his cabin drinking steaming coffee, he spotted an antelope across the lake. It would be a real treat. Save the occasional rabbit, which only made for a decent stew, fresh meat in winter was a rare meal indeed. Brown put on his coat and pulled on his mukluks. He grabbed his rifle from where it stood near the door, leapt from the cabin and strode across the clearing to the water's edge. He stopped short when a voice called to him.

"Kootenai, I hope you don't have eyes on my antelope over yonder!"

Brown turned around.

"Jack Street, I'll be damned! What brings you out here on this awful cold day?"

"Parcel came into town for you. Felt like a ride in the crisp air," he explained. "Couple of miles east of here, I picked up the trail of that fine buck over there."

"Let's divvy him up, then," replied Brown.

Street dismounted, and the pair walked across the frozen river towards the far side of the lake where the antelope was standing. Suddenly, Kootenai fell straight down. In a split second, only his head and one hand, clutched desperately to the edge of the hole in the ice, were visible.

"Damn it Jack!" Kootenai hollered. "The current's pulling hard. She's sucking me in!"

Street moved quickly. Flat on his belly, he reached towards his friend. He didn't want to get too close for fear of the ice cracking. If he joined Kootenai in the water, he'd be of no help to either of them. The only thing he had to extend to Kootenai was his rifle.

"Grab hold of the barrel!" Street cried, his own hands tight on its butt.

Kootenai lifted his hand out of the water and gripped the rifle. His wet leather mitten stuck to the cold metal and allowed him to hold tight. Slowly, Street began to edge backwards. It was demanding work, but soon Kootenai was able to kick free of the hole.

"Never thought I'd be so happy to see the business end of Hawkens," Kootenai chattered.

Street laughed, pulled off his coat and wrapped it around his friend. They hurriedly made their way back to the cabin. Kootenai's wife had observed the near disaster, and already had the whisky poured. Kootenai stripped down, put on some warm clothes and raised a cup to his friend in thanks.

In the spring following Kootenai's near drowning, he and Street, who had since retired from the North-West Mounted Police, were hired as guides for a party of hunters out of Fort Macleod. The pair had built their reputation on being able to find animals in any season, and rare was the sportsman who returned home without a story to tell and wild meat for dinner. When the trio of hunters arrived at Kootenai's cabin, they received an enthusiastic welcome.

"Boys, I hope you brought the elephant rifles," smiled Kootenai. "I got a feeling we're going to see some big game! And, from the looks of it, there's plenty to go around, so I hope you brought lots of ammo, too."

There was little better way of starting off a hunting trip than with such words of encouragement, and as Kootenai loaded up the packhorses, the hunters bubbled with excitement. The snow had melted considerably over the past few weeks, and traveling was easy. They made their way along the Kootenay River, swinging west just beyond the upper reaches of the middle lake. The route allowed them to bypass the many small streams that fed the lake—no sense in taking any more chances with risky ice.

"There she is, boys," pointed Street. "Mount Boswell, named after a fellow in the British Boundary Commission a few years back."

"Boswell, hell," grumbled Kootenai. He hated the fact that European names were replacing the traditional Native ones. It took away from the history of the place.

The men began to set up camp. Shortly, the tents were up, and a fire was burning nicely. The sun was low in the sky.

"Boys, it's too late to hunt today, so we'll make a start of it tomorrow," said Kootenai, as he settled in near the fire.

"I'm going to head over to the mountain and see if I can pick up any sign of game," said Street.

As the men relaxed around the fire, Kootenai asked for something a little stronger than coffee and began to tell the men a story about a white buffalo he had once seen. He was describing his attempt to sneak up on the animal by still hunting, hunting without the use of his horse, when he heard a low rumble just within earshot. Suddenly, a rifle cracked. Kootenai looked up, his eyes immediately drawn to the source of the noise. He saw Jack Street, away in the distance, on the side of Mount Boswell. His friend was waving his arms. Seconds later, Jack was swallowed by an avalanche rolling down the side of the mountain.

Kootenai was off with uncommon speed. The hunting party followed at a distance. When they arrived at the base of the mountain, Kootenai was already digging wildly. They could all see that the situation was hopelesss, though the opinion went unspoken. Instead, they joined Kootenai. Under the light of the full moon, they dug into the late hours of the night. Finally, one of the men spoke the words no one wanted to hear.

"He's dead, Kootenai. No one could still be alive."

Kootenai collapsed on the snow. In a rare sign of emotion, he let out a wail that pierced the night. Eventually, he joined the others, and they slowly made their way back to camp.

Kootenai returned to the mountain later that spring, when the last of the snows had melted. Already, the peak was known as Street Mountain. He began to climb and eventually stumbled upon a crevice that was barely visible from the ground. Deep in its belly was Jack Street's body. There was no way to retrieve the corpse, and even if there had been, Kootenai wasn't of a mind to move it. The spot served as his friend's final resting place.

The tragedy turned Kootenai's thoughts to more serious matters. He joined the Theosophical Society, a spiritual

On the border between Canada and the United States in
Alberta, Waterton Lakes National Park (originally Kootenay
Lakes Forest Reserve) was created because of the determination
of Kootenai Brown and a handful of other conservationists.
Brown first set eyes on the inspiring landscape in 1865, and
although he didn't return there for more than a decade, the
beauty of crystalline lakes, rolling hills and soaring mountains
was never far from his thoughts. By the 1890s he was a vocal
advocate for the preservation of the region. He wanted
controls placed on exploitation of its natural resources and
encouraged the adoption of policies that would attract
visitors. Brown was rewarded for his efforts in 1895 when the
Canadian government established the forest reserve. He was
none too pleased when the government renamed the reserve
Waterton Lakes National Park. Its namesake, Charles Waterton,
had never even been to Alberta, and Brown preferred that
the name remain Native. The park currently encompasses
205 square miles.

organization that emphasized a personal relationship with nature. As he entered his 60s, when most folks were enjoying a slower pace, he threw his shoulder into a matter that had long interested him, the conservation of the Kootenay Lakes region. During the last 15 years of his life, Kootenai took on several jobs for the Dominion government's civil service, all of them related to the protection and promotion of his home.

Kootenai was at the forefront of efforts to preserve the region. He was worried when he saw the first oil companies build their rigs in the early 1890s, and he joined with prominent local ranchers and politicians to pressure the government into protecting the area. Although the government was more interested in the financial gains of resource development than it was in conservation, over the years, the dogged efforts of Kootenai and his friends saw the small Kootenay Forest Reserve, a picnic grounds created in 1895, grow to a national park of some 425 square miles by 1914.

During those years, Kootenai served as a fisheries officer, game guardian and forestry ranger. The physical demands of the jobs were staggering. Kootenai rode 250 miles a month. In the winter, he stabled his horse and donned snowshoes. And finally, in his early 70s, he mastered the typewriter!

Kootenai also took pleasure in serving as the park's public relations man. He wrote letters describing the beauty of the region to organizations and newspapers; he made certain that conditions were suitable for tourists; and he pressured the Dominion government for changes that would enhance the park's usability, such as reducing the $1 camping fee. Many a visitor enjoyed a mug-up with Brown, who would often arrive unexpectedly at their camp with a story or two of the old days to tell.

He also oversaw commercial developments. Kootenai rarely opposed the businesses that sought to exploit the region's resources, but he was insistent that they be regulated and not infringe upon the region's natural beauty.

Kootenai was upset when the Dominion government changed the name of the Kootenay Forest Reserve to Waterton Lakes National Park in 1911. Charles Waterton, its namesake, had never even been to Canada. Kootenai considered the change to be an example of modern officialdom at its worst and a slight to the region's true history. He predicted that the Natives would all soon enough be killed off or so mixed up with the white folks that they might as well be dead. He wasn't happy about the changes, but as a realist, he also believed their fate inevitable.

As he once revealed to a friend, "In the march of civilization, the buffalo had to go and so did the Indian. There's no place for their way of life in this new world."

He thought that the names Natives left behind would be the settlers' only memory of them and that they were worth maintaining.

When the park was expanded in 1914, the authorities considered Kootenai too old to handle the new position of superintendent. But Kootenai continued to offer his advice to his new boss and to carry out his patrols as a ranger even though the long rides of yesteryear were a fading memory. In 1913, he sold his homestead and moved to Fort Macleod, where he enjoyed great popularity with the children who loved to listen to his stories. But Kootenay was slowing down and was often ill. He turned to whiskey for its medicinal effects, but it brought none of the pleasure of gallons swilled long ago. He cursed Isabella for watering the hooch down, and she rightfully protested her innocence. The whiskey wasn't losing its kick; Kootenai was losing his. He died on July 18, 1916.